THE REALIZATION OF DEATH

THE HUMANIZATION OF DEATH

Avery D. Weisman, M.D.

The Realization of Death

*A Guide
for the
Psychological
Autopsy*

with a foreword by EDWIN S. SHNEIDMAN, Ph.D.

Jason Aronson   *New York, London*

LIBRARY OF CONGRESS CATALOGING IN PUBLICATION DATA

Weisman, Avery D
    The realization of death.
    Bibliography: p.
    1. Death—Psychology. 2. Suicide. I. Title.
[DNLM: 1. Attitude to death. 2. Death. BF789. D4
W428r 1974]
BF789.D4W37   616   74-8343
ISBN 0-87668-163-1

Designed by Sidney Solomon
Manufactured in the United States of America

Think of me—once in a while.

ANONYMOUS EPITAPH

CONTENTS

Foreword

I have advertently never checked Dr. Weisman's chronological age—I believe him to be a few years older than I am—but, probably on the grounds of his wisdom and maturity of mind and character, I think of him psychologically as a father, not avuncular, certainly not sibling, but as an ageless parent: giving, fair, a preceptor, a perfect friend.

It now comes as an unexampled opportunity in my own life to be asked by him to write a Foreword to a book written largely around an idea which was, so to speak, a child of mine. At least, even if there was multiple conception, I witnessed the delivery, I named the offspring, and attended the early birthday ceremonies. There is nothing so sweet in intellectual life as having one's ideas taken seriously by first-rate others.

The psychological autopsy is no longer an infant. It comes of age in Dr. Weisman's book. The special features of the psychological autopsy lie in its multidisciplinary spirit, the involvement of several stripes of social and behavioral scientists in the retrospective creation, from as many sources as possible, of the tangible features of a now-dead fellow human—to bring him to "life" as it were—and then try to divine his motivations, intentions, attitudes, and ambivalences in relation to one specific temporal span of behavior which in itself had extreme consequences—his dying. Dr. Weisman aptly terms this the "focal event."

In the history of the psychological autopsy, Dr. Theodore J. Curphey, then Chief Medical Examiner-Coroner of Los Angeles County, has to be cited as perhaps the most important element in its early growth and acceptance. Without his active endorsement and participation on real cases, where real issues of equivocality of death were recognized, the idea might still exist only somewhere alphabetically under the category, a priori. He was the godfather of the psychological autopsy, in the genuine sense of the word.

But it was Dr. Weisman who adopted, nurtured, and brought it to present fruition in this very book. He is a thanatologist, one of the most difficult of medical/behavioral science specialties to practice. Working with dying people, helping them toward an "appropriate death"—Dr. Weisman's felicitous phrase—is psychologically depleting and abrasive, because it touches upon man's mortalities. Even the thanatologist is, after all, only superhuman.

Dr. Weisman is more than a thanatologist. Perhaps because of or as a result of what he is, physician, psychiatrist, psychoanalyst, he is in this book existential minister, occupational counselor, and even psychotherapist for all thanatologists who need his services. And that group, while small in actual numbers

—how many people refer to themselves as thanatologists?—is vast in practice. Almost every physician, most clergymen, social workers, nurses, attorneys
who deal with loss, bereavement, and the grief of others
are unofficial thanatologists. Every sympathetic citizen
whose best elements resonate to the crushing needs of
others cannot help but respond to the issues Dr. Weisman describes in this book. He is correct beyond measure when he says that the psychological autopsy is not
merely for the professional, but for anyone who would
come to a fuller realization of death.

His extended and moving case vignettes are better
than fiction, teaching us as only real cases can. The
imaginative application of Dr. Henry Murray's Thematic Apperception Test adds an extra dimension to the
case reports. Most of all, I think, Dr. Weisman's
humane, yet strict and compelling, adherence to actual
cases does not allow the reader latitude for escapist
sentimentality or generalization.

In the 1950s and 60s, psychological autopsies were
used at the Los Angeles Suicide Prevention Center,
working in conjunction with the Los Angeles County
Coroner's Office. We adopted it as a means of classifying
equivocal deaths—was a death suicide or accident?

Dr. Weisman has creatively extended the reach of
the psychological autopsy to deaths that are unequivocal as to mode, pursuing such additional piercing
questions as: Why did this (clearly physical, accidental,
or suicidal) death occur at *this* time? What psychological events preceding the dying period might be related
to the death itself? How can we understand this death
better? In short, he has done the work of any modest
genius. He has asked the obvious questions and then

proceeded to provide data and reflections relevant to their answers.

Perhaps I have already dwelt too much on the personal relationship between Dr. Weisman and me, so that you can see why I cannot simply bless him for this book. He blesses me in having written it, and permitting me to write this Foreword. But I can also thank him for this bounty of ideas, clinical insights, intimate sharing, human wisdom, and guide to the seeds of courage that lie in us all in relation to our own mortality.

In one place, while discussing a suicidal patient, Dr. Weisman states, "I can predict almost anything —except the future." Well, I think that I can safely predict the reception of this book. It will be welcomed by all who think about the dying condition. It flows easily, moves smoothly, and will be read avidly by everyone who wonders and puzzles over what his own death will be like.

I once said that Dr. Weisman was a man I would be willing to die with, thinking that was the ultimate compliment of trust and regard. Now I see that I can append something else: I would be willing to have him do my psychological autopsy.

—*Edwin S. Shneidman, Ph.D.*

Los Angeles, California

THE REALIZATION OF DEATH

Chapter 1

INTRODUCTION

This is not an essay on death, of which there are already too many. It is primarily designed to be a guide, not an exhaustive treatise, for professionals who would undertake the venture, emotional and scientific, of more completely assessing death and dying, especially as found in a general hospital. But the *realization of death* is not confined to professional specialties: it is the common destiny of every culture and every person who would try to make sense out of his own individuality.

Realization has two meanings: to perceive a reality, and to make real. Neither occurs without the other. In the instance of death and dying, although they are by no means identical, we are always haunted by awareness of our time-limited existence. Nevertheless, we readily, gladly postpone, put aside, disavow, and deny its relevance for us. Consequently, death as a personal experience is extruded from our field of reality and realization, until, of course, sooner or later, it thrusts back upon our consciousness. As a rule, we perpetuate self-deception through comfortable platitudes, assigning the task of confronting death to certain professionals in our society. Few people are willing to accept death as a topic to be directly and dispassionately investigated. Most people concede that death is inevitable, a fact of nature. But they are not prepared to *realize*, in the double sense I indicated, that death can be systematically explored, and thereby, much of its inherent dread can be attenuated.

Living and dying are two phases of the same psychobiological process, which starts at birth—or before—and continues throughout innumerable stages until cessation—or beyond. We recognize various facts, facets, and problems of life and death with different portions of acceptance and denial. We cope with dilemmas, conflicts, and crises with a mixture of success, defeat, compromise, irresolution, and vulnerability. But none of us is entirely free of a deep fear of death, or exempt from dread of annihilation. Even without knowing a dead person, or having any information about how he lived or died, the mere presence of a dead body before us evokes emotional repercussions.

The anatomical autopsy which is practiced today discloses only organic remains. Strangely enough, many medical professionals have but a fleeting knowledge of human pathology as demonstrated by an autopsy. It is not unusual, furthermore, to meet highly educated, cultured, and worldly wise men and women who would literally shudder at the notion of touching a dead body, let alone watching a dissection. These may be people who are sensitive to the problems and woes of mankind, who do not customarily shelter themselves from other grim facts.

Dissection of a dead body, however, shows only the deleterious result of disease, injury, poisoning. But no matter how meticulously the autopsy be performed, or how sophisticated the analysis of organs and body fluids, we never learn "who" the someone was that is now the dead body. To name but a few examples, we may know what he died of, not what he lived for—his self-awareness, style of life, success or failure, personal relationships, good or bad, aspirations, despairs.

Even the anatomical autopsy has come under question these days. Why, then, should we study the psychological and sociological aspects of death-related situations and life-threatening behavior? How can we justify the expenditure of talent and energy necessary for the psychological autopsy?

I can only answer that unless we understand more about the psychosocial dimensions of life and death, as shown through individual cases, we ignore the human side of being alive. Moreover, we will not appreciate what it signifies for someone to become ill, then —instead of recovering—to become very ill, to decline and deteriorate, relinquishing presence and autonomy, more distressed and debilitated, until reaching the ultimate fact of sickness unto death.

Brain dissections show brain anatomy; nothing of the personality. Autopsies demonstrate pathological anatomy; nothing of a person's feelings, thoughts, desires, and dreads. It is merely an abstraction to say that someone died of a disease. Death is so much a part of the human condition that to assign causes to why someone dies is almost an artificiality. Die we must, whether by accident, intention, allotment, or decrepitude. We tend to separate the fact of death from its origin—how one dies, with whom, when, where, and all the things one dies to in the course of terminality. Everything ceases with death. In the process of dying, however, images and perceptions change, relationships and emotions shift, even the field of human interaction twists and narrows, shrinking into a tiny capsule of preoccupation. Trivial episodes and casual events which ordinarily would get little notice may assume magnified proportions. In a similar way, simple bodily functions and acts become tests of independence as well as measures of increasing disability.

Every question affecting mankind involves death. It is an answer to many of the ultimate questions that most people find hard to formulate. Our cultural heritage has largely given us only methods to deny, romanticize, and placate death, and very little that can be used to understand the meaning and mechanisms of dying. Modern man, however, has faced death more directly and more frequently than have other generations. Whereas once we might limit the world to that in our immediate vicinity, communications across oceans and intercontinental space bring events into our homes, and depict catastrophes and calamities in ways that breach denial and romance. People are more aware of death than they once were. They are dissatisfied with global pronouncements, comfortable platitudes, and ceremonial supports that their forebears scarcely questioned. In seeking to make sense out of life, many people, particularly of the younger generations, sometimes turn away from traditional disciplines, including science. Instead, they yield to the promises of certainty offered by the irrational forces in life and death. It is as if heightened awareness of death hastens a search for capturing the "essence" of life—whatever that is.

Immediate experience in the here-and-now does offer a measure of personal enrichment, but we also need the foundations of what we know from the past and foresee in the future. Unfortunately, we also carry the baggage of superstition and preconceptions.

The enigmas of existence certainly cannot be solved simply by dispassionately examining the psychosocial dimensions and stages of death and dying. But if death and dying are inevitable phases of human experience, then it is necessary to find ways to fathom what it means to be alive and to be alive to. Members of the health professions are perplexed, and like most people, find solace in certainty, particularly in situations about which no one can be sure. Modern medicine, a term that conjures up visions of antibiotic triumphs, twisted molecules, and technological wizardry, has still not fully realized that the terminal phase of life needs more investigation. The very facts that have brought healing into being—facts of life and death—have prevented the healing professions from responding to deep yearning to know more about death and deadliness in human nature.

Medicine's claim to be the science and art of healing may be partially responsible for avoiding the reality of death as a legitimate subject for scientific inquiry. Rational medicine seeks to ameliorate disease by finding its causes and reversing its effects. But we should look further, because medicine has only recently—as such things are measured—begun to be rational. There is a mystical and magical tradition which is far more ancient. Medicine has always dealt with the mysteries of life and death. Part of its awesome authority stems from the proximity to disease and sickness. To define medicine as the science and art of healing is simply another way of seeking to postpone and circumvent recognition of death. We can deny its reality, minimize its probability; then if every strategy is insufficient, forswear our part.

Like most human beings, physicians and other members of the health professions—"healers"—are afraid of death. Hence, it was a milestone for humanity when medicine could first autonomously examine facts of fatal illness, without recourse to dogmatism and tradition. In doing so, however, it was necessary to isolate physical factors in death from the personal.

Thanatology, the study of death, dying, bereavement, life-threatening behavior, and suicide, developed out of the scientific tradition and an even longer heritage of service and compassion. During the past decade or two, starting with Feifel's book, *The Meaning of Death* (1959), publications about death and dying have proliferated enormously. More articles and books have appeared than their substance justifies. The public wants more, but disciplined observations and scientific investigation of specific problems are still in short supply.

My purpose in writing about the psychological autopsy is not, of course, to close the door on further investigation of death. Nor would I insist that psychological autopsies are the only way to find out more about dying and deathly situations. Indeed, the psychological autopsy, as it stands, is a very crude instrument. It may, however, open other doors for more systematic explorations of death.

Medicine knows a great deal about disease, but very little about the manner in which people die. The autopsy helps disclose reasons for death, but very little about the self within the cadaver, who lived and died,

moved and was moved, within a tiny web of relationships. Even the term "autopsy," the postmortem examination of a dead body, overlooks its stem, *autos*, the
self.

Death is still a forbidden topic. While enjoying
popularity at present, fascination with death reflects a
strategy which helps counter the awe, fear, and rever-
ence usually felt. Death is always perceived ambiva-
lently; it is mixture of the sacred and the sinister. Taboos
about the dead are not limited to primitive peoples.
Even professionals avoid talking about death, and
imply that beyond a point of distance and impersonal-
ity, studying death can itself become a deadly business.

This book is dedicated to the dispassionate investigation of death-related situations, especially as en-
countered by the patient facing imminent, intended, or
incipient death. Dispassion does not mean impersonal-
ity or disinvolvement. Rather, it is the gentle neutrality
of quiet dignity, seeking to learn, to understand, to
participate. The suicidal patient certainly merits equal
concern and study. The waste of human life exacted by
self-imposed destruction defeats humanity itself. However, physicians and other clinicians are less hesitant to
talk with people about suicide attempts than about
death and dying. These inquiries will not violate privacy, threaten stability, or hasten a patient's demise.
Candid discussion does not make any patient worse.
Nevertheless, some physicians, skillful but uneasy
about human conflicts and bringing bad tidings, still
believe that confrontations can be harmful—a notion
based not on experience, but on the anxiety and dread
aroused by transgression of a primitive taboo. Inexora-
ble death so pervades life that it generates qualms in

almost everyone touched by its shadow. For these reasons and others, we search for better methods, more information about this critical phase. We seek information, not more intimidation. Touched by fear, we want to relieve people of the contamination of ignorance and dogmatism.

Much of the information and many of the examples on which this book is based come from our work in *Project Omega*. In its first phase, Project Omega was a psychological autopsy study of terminal illness and suicide. It was funded from 1968 until 1972 by the Center for Studies of Suicide Prevention, National Institute of Mental Health. In its second phase, our research moved away from the terminal phase of life to the study of how cancer patients cope and fail to cope during the initial stage of their illness. This work has been supported by the National Cancer Institute, which believes that cancer treatment cannot be confined to the treatment of tumors, but of people, as well.

The link between coping with cancer and the terminal phase of life should not be misunderstood. How cancer patients cope with psychosocial concerns may, of course, anticipate how some patients will accommodate to terminal illness. However, it is false to believe, as many people do, that cancer is the prototype of fatal illness. Despite educational campaigns and medical progress, these people persist in being less afraid of illnesses with a far worse prognosis than cancer. This fact itself shows that psychosocial forces begin to operate in the prediagnostic stages of illness, and certainly continue throughout its course. Principles, precepts, and knowledge derived from a study of terminal patients may be applicable to the initial care of patients who will not die of that illness. However, since death is our common fate, anything we learn during psychological autopsies could be the basis for larger generalizations about human behavior during the crisis of sickness and sickness to death.

Although I have been principal investigator for Project Omega in its psychological autopsy phase (Omega I) and in its cancer-coping phase (Omega II), the core staff, headed by J. William Worden, Ph.D., Research Director, has done most of the work, far more than even the case illustrations indicate. No statement of appreciation would adequately convey my indebtedness and gratitude. Only they know, as I hope the reader will, the frustrations and satisfactions that can be generated by psychological autopsy sessions and preparations. For those who see that a disciplined study of death needs more than theories, and that care of the dying needs more than compassion, this work is intended.

Chapter 2

PRINCIPLES

Scope of Thanatology

During a clinicopathological conference (CPC), I often muse about what the patient under discussion might say on his own behalf, were he suddenly resurrected and asked about his final illness. If he quietly entered the room and sat in the back, how long would it be before he even recognized himself, amid anatomical findings, laboratory reports, and technical jargon?

He might, of course, be very gratified that efforts expended on diagnosis, testing, and treatment were so thorough, even though he did not survive. His death did provide instruction for doctors which might be useful in treating other patients. He might also be puzzled, even amazed, to discover that his frail body contained such esoteric aberrations and pathological conditions. In any event, he would learn that from a very ordinary human being, he had been transformed into an "interesting case."

But he could also be a bit dismayed. In the passage from health to sickness, then from sickness to death, he

11

has become a specimen and a statistic. So he might not be reassured because he left some interesting remains for doctors to ponder. In fact, it is not he that is interesting, but the disease. What, then, happened to him?

From the standpoint of the CPC, the patient's reflections might be quite irrelevant. But suppose we ask this recently revived specimen a few questions, anyway.

"Sir [I do not know his name], how did you feel when you first became ill? What did you think was wrong? After the tests were done and the treatments didn't seem to help, what was it like? What more did you expect? Who spoke to you about the sickness or about the next part of the treatment? What did you ask? What did your doctor say about how things were coming along? Did he hint that you might not get better, that you might get worse, never go back to work or return to your family?

"When and how did you first realize that you could die, or in fact, were dying? What bothered or concerned you most about this outcome? To whom could you talk? What did you say? Assuming that you might have chosen to die—although it seems hard to believe —would it have been here, now, under these circumstances?

"How much help were your family and friends? Did they stay and talk with you, reassure you, cry, make bad jokes, or just keep their distance? How did you reconcile yourself to what was coming—I mean death? If you could do it over again, what would you have done differently?

"What about your doctor? Was he straightforward, or a little too evasive, too technical, too sad himself, or too something else? One more question, Sir. If we had met before now, could I have been of any help? How?"

These imaginary questions refer to the psychosocial dimensions of death. They are imaginary only because there is no limit to the social and psychological intricacies of disease, dying, and death. When we think about the limitless questions which could be asked, it is shocking that as a rule we have such sketchy information about this aspect of illness and mortality.

Obviously, there is much more about disease and death than can be revealed by the most searching autopsy and CPC. Except in the most limited physicalistic sense, questions about how and why anyone dies when he does are simply not asked. If the ghost of the patient were to answer, however, it is likely that he would not focus on organic issues, but on the personal plight of someone who became ill and then died. The autopsy eliminates interpersonal and intrapersonal elements so completely and strategically that we scarcely notice their absence. Even seasoned physicians shrink away from the personal reality of a death in which they have been involved. To some doctors, death is a sign of failure, a flaw in the power with which they have been endowed. Why?

Death is inevitable, but physicians still maintain that survival in almost any form or under any conditions is better than oblivion. Death is natural, but even the easiest death seems to epitomize dread and terror. Dissolution, termination, extinction are frightening. So we keep our distance until the personal impact has diluted. Then we can deal with death and dying as medical abstractions—no longer the death of this man, or that woman.

The scope of thanatology covers the entire range of death-related situations and life-threatening behavior—terminal illness, suicide, bereavement, fatal injury and intoxication, and so forth. The psychological autopsy, however, is one method of appraising the psychosocial dimensions of death and deadly events, however we choose to define them. Logically, the psychological autopsy is an extension of the anatomical. Historically, the anatomical autopsy is a specialized method of appraising the generics of death from the organic viewpoint.

The Organic Tradition

Scientific medicine could scarcely exist without the organic tradition that "anatomy is everything." Sickness is due to physical illness; physical illness, to a disease; and disease leaves its marks on various organs, invariably in their disturbed functions. Some diseases cannot be correlated with specific lesions. Nevertheless, the organic tradition insists that with delicate enough methods and techniques, subanatomical lesions might be found, even in aberrations of protein molecules.

The autopsy and CPC—let us regard them as one procedure for convenience—make use of bedside observations, clinical constructions, diagnoses, physical and physiological principles, and postmortem information. The combined intelligence of the assembled specialists then determines the pathological processes that presumably led to death.

Any problem that falls outside this circle of procedures and type of data is not of primary concern to the organic tradition. Information about the social network, personal behavior, relationships, economic status, emotional style, and so forth is therefore not available, because tradition decides that it is not important. We can find out what a patient died with, in terms of organic remains, rarely what he died from, and never what he lived for—his sense of purpose, even how he managed to live at all in the midst of turbulent and threatening times.

Medical practice still contains many elements of mystery, magic, sorcery, and authoritarianism. Our style of practice usually runs far ahead of scientific knowledge and established principles; recent controversies about informed consent and the patient's right to know also suggest that at times our practice has even exceeded social conscience.

The autopsy/CPC is a stabilizing influence derived from the organic tradition. It stimulates medical conscience, or self-scrutiny by physicians, and generates scientific information. Without it, we might fall back upon the magical side of medicine, and revert to the practices that flourished during the Middle Ages, supported by superstition, fear of heresy, and philosophical preconceptions.

Nevertheless, the organic tradition itself can become stultified. The autopsy is questioned by many authorities, as if it had reached the limit of useful information. It is also likely that too much emphasis upon tangible remnants of disease may impede other questions we might ask about illness, dying, and death. Obviously, an autopsy room should not be a theater in which a gifted clinician displays his legerdemain. Nor should it be a "Stump the Experts" show for the pathologist who has all the answers. A very rare case may be striking, and at times, instructive, but it is questionable what a practitioner can be expected to learn from such exotic fauna.

There are some diseases for which no dissectable lesions exist. More importantly, some patients manage to survive far longer and with fewer symptoms than do other patients with the same disease and who have received similar treatments. Organic pathology cannot explain the reasons for this disparity. Moreover, while everyone must die of something someday, we are not always sure—to put it gently—why they die when they do, and why they have symptoms or lack of symptoms.

In 1967, Feinstein proposed that the key to disease and its complications, as well as its outcome, is not wholly a problem of delicate differential diagnosis, that standby of a proficient physician. A more accurate indicator would be certain sets of symptoms which provide the basis for differential prognosis. Feinstein also suggested that we think about diagnosis, disease, and illness as different entities which follow quasi-independent rules. For example, the same diagnosis may refer to several diseases showing widely differing behavior. Thus, if disease is not accurately designated by that cultural convention called diagnosis, then illness, the subjective state, may not, and usually does not, follow an identical course, and should be separated from concepts of disease and diagnosis. People can and do become sick, even die, in different ways and at different times, despite having the same diagnostic labels and clinical findings.

This observation is not really very bold. In fact, it is so common that scarcely anyone pauses to wonder why it is true. Statistical variation in morbidity and mortality from various diseases/diagnoses are not explanations for illness and its effects. Basically, it is the individual (some people call it biological activity) who counts. We can call it protoplasm, personality, and psychosocial predicaments.

Weed has advocated wider use of the Problem-Oriented Record (POR), a format that enables a physician to list major presenting clinical problems when he first examines a patient, and then to plot out the methods of investigating those problems. The POR is not a solution to any problem but that of slavish adherence to the organic tradition. It might, however, broaden the perspective of medical diagnosis and treatment to include problems which transcend the anatomical and biochemical.

Only an unrepentant spiritualist would do away with the organic tradition, to which we owe so much. As Weed points out, however, the autopsy/CPC can be used more effectively than at present, when the pathologist is expected to be the final arbiter of every baffling clinical problem. He proposes that the autopsy become a station at which certain findings and formulations can be tested, instead of the final destination of every medical task that goes wrong. Moreover, he urges medicine to expand its data from a narrow concept of disease, what is objectively found, to a broad view of illness, what a patient complains about.

The essential idea behind the POR is to bring in and to call upon other professionals who participate in the care of patients. Weed suggests that paramedical professionals and specialists without primary responsibility for the patient do, nevertheless, have much to contribute. To the extent that they observe and formulate salient problems pertaining to the sick person, these people have methods and data that might help solve problems of other kinds.

The contributions of Weed, Feinstein, Goldfinger, and others deserve to be heeded because, regardless of the merits of the POR, their aim is to expand our thinking about medical logic and clinical problems. The organic viewpoint is, naturally, here to stay. There is still room for better comprehension of how illness begins and ends, including the personal issues in being sick or fatally ill.

The Psychosocial Viewpoint

How and why people become ill requires both technical information and concepts broad enough to admit nonorganic data. Medicine is not an exact science, but a set of socially sanctioned disciplines. At what point, therefore, do we accept certain kinds of information and discard others as irrelevant, unscientific, or immaterial? Certain disciplines are more objective and operational. Others stem from social customs and traditions, untested and often unformulated. For example, most doctors do not realize that in following the organic model of illness they are Cartesian dualists who rigidly separate the tangibility of the body from the ideas of the mind. The reigning hierarchy of medicine decrees, therefore, that the physician is best equipped to treat a patient because he presumably knows most about the disease. Information about psychosocial matters (which the physician usually knows little about) is disregarded, or thought to amount to mere "epi-phenomena," i.e., irrelevant adornments of the clinical history. All that remains is the diagnosis, which then determines what happens to the patient thereafter.

The concept of diagnosis is admittedly unsatisfactory. It is derived from the organic tradition that reaches back into antiquity and Hippocrates. After all, what is a "diagnosis"? It has three parts: a name for an organic disorder, what a doctor does to explain a patient's complaints, and a method of management. In brief, diagnosis is not simply a set of terms, but a series of problem-solving assessments.

Social workers, nurses, physiotherapists, psychologists, and so forth may understand much more about how a patient actually feels, thinks, and behaves than do the physicians who are formally in charge of that patient. But the organic tradition and hierarchy decrees that this kind of information—psychosocial data—is not particularly significant. The relevance of emotional factors in physical illness needs no argument. But in everyday transactions, psychosocial factors are not considered to be critical issues.

Illness is far too important to be left to physicians. In fact, treatment of seriously ill patients is seldom carried out only by physicians. Nurses and other professionals carry out "doctor's orders," but in reality, they do the ministrations and management. Their services are not merely the obedient reflexes of a trained servant, but an outcome based upon separate disciplined studies. The primary physician may, in fact, know very little about the patient or the illness, because he emphasizes the diagnosis. Other hospital staff respond to complaints, administer medicine, carry out procedures, observe results, talk with families, and, in short, implement, if not entirely originate, policies for care.

This situation is particularly conspicuous in cases of fatal illness. Some doctors believe that unless it is they who tell, or decide not to tell, a patient about diagnosis and proposed treatment, no information will be transmitted. The patient will, it is assumed, not be told, nor will he draw any conclusions. An absurdity, but scarcely as absurd as not telling a patient anything, hoping that he will thereby know nothing. Seriously ill patients know much more than we imagine, far more than they have been told, and certainly more than they ask about.

Illness is part of the human condition. Every disease, injury, or incapacity has psychosocial implications. We may not, however, have adequate language and instruments to detect the degree of illness according to psychosocial criteria. On rounds one day, a group of physicians found that an aged, arthritic woman patient had developed an acute inflammation of her eyes, with bilateral conjunctivitis and lacrimation. They discussed possible etiologies of this condition, especially in relation to joint swelling. Then a nurse interrupted to explain that on the day before, the patient learned of the sudden death of her sister, and had been crying.

On one hand, this curious episode reflects professionalized preoccupation with the physical. Tears are "lacrimation," not signs of sorrow. But on the other hand, the patient's plight could not be described in language other than assuming that her sister's death precipitated red, swollen, tearful eyes. The relation between them, why the patient did not mention her loss, and a host of intervening variables between a psychosocial event and physiological responsiveness still need to be understood more precisely. Why, for example, do personal losses have such different effects? Recent theories of depression show that sadness and sorrow, hopelessness, and helplessness cover a wide range of clinical situations, some of which are evidently learned, others, reinforced, and still others, the product of biogenic amines.

In any case, it is inevitable that unless psychosocial disciplines develop their own language and instruments, the organic viewpoint will prevail. When this occurs, the universe is utterly mechanistic; the sick person is a body of malfunctioning misery. The body consists of a set of abstractions, in which the heart is an electric pump, the liver is a chemical laboratory, the kidney is a drainage system, and the brain is a computer.

Illness involves social, emotional, moral, economic, and existential concerns, beside those covered by the organic. Psychiatric theories, terminology, and investigative methods are insufficient to account for how various patients cope with illness. Psychosocial factors contribute both to the fact of illness and to the decisions we make about patients who are ill. Sometimes, a patient brings aberrant behavior with him into the hospital. But at other times, hospital environments create aberrant and unacceptable behavior. Illness does not consist simply of physical aberrance, but is a psychosocial upheaval in itself. Some years ago, Hackett and Weisman found that existing psychiatric nomenclature—neurosis, psychosis, character disorders—failed to describe the range of social and emotional responses found among surgical patients, before and after operation. They urged that psychiatric consultants participate more actively in formulating and carrying out their interventions. Their "psychotherapeutic consultation" anticipated the problem-oriented record. In their view, but updating their terminology, psychiatrists would be much more useful if psychosocial guidance systems were developed. Pathogenic forces and events could be identified, problems formulated, and appropriate solutions sought.

The psychosocial viewpoint is neither a theory nor an alternative treatment modality. Very simply, it is an effort to gather more information about a sick patient, but in the direction of how he adapts to illness and maintains equilibrium in the presence of social, economic, emotional disruptions.

There are many blank pages in the chronicles of illness, physical and emotional. The psychosocial viewpoint is a way to identify the uniqueness of a clinical situation in which a patient finds himself, yet with sufficient generality to be applicable to other patients. Psychiatrists are often rebuked for being outside the mainstream of medicine, a charge which is not altogether false. But physicians are also called upon daily to make psychosocial assessments, more often than they need to undertake exhaustive laboratory diagnostic tests. That they do not realize the innate presence of psychosocial forces in illness only underscores how easily they slip into using commonsense conjectures, half-truths, moralisms, and unwarranted universal dicta.

All that the psychological autopsy method assumes is that illness is not wholly an organic matter, but a manifestation of impersonal, interpersonal, and intrapersonal forces impinging upon people within a psychobiological medium.

The Psychological Autopsy Method

Mention the "psychological autopsy" to most physicians, and their first response will be bewilderment, amusement, or just plain disbelief. "How can you do an "autopsy" on anything so intangible as the mind—isn't that what *psychological* means?"

The term is paradoxical, but the method only seems unthinkable because we are not accustomed to thinking about what is meant by mind or by the autopsy. Without getting into the various meanings of mental events, the mind refers simply to anything we are mindful of, and this includes whatever can be perceived, thought about, and acted upon. Autopsy, as already defined, means something more than postmortem dissection of remains. After all, what are the "remains" but a person who is no longer alive, after the humanity has been distilled away?

Most societies have taboos about dead bodies, and ours is no exception. Rituals and special ceremonies separate the living from the dead, and the latter especially includes the recently deceased whose spirits are thought to hover in the vicinity.

The organic tradition splits the person into mind and body, the personality from its container, or, if you wish, the soul from the soma. Rational medicine depends upon the inviolability of the split. It is probably not a coincidence that *regular* postmortem examination

of dead bodies did not take place with anything re-
sembling scientific precision until the rise of
rationalism in the eighteenth century. Whether belief in
witchcraft or the stringent dictates of canon law helped
to advance studies of anatomy or to establish reasons
for suspicious deaths is a question best left to historians.
In 1507, however, Benivieni published a posthumous
work reporting twenty autopsies. Bonet (1679) is considered to be the forerunner of Morgagni and Linné,
pathologists whose major works were published almost
a century later.

For generations, old sanctions and even older fears
prohibited physicians from dissecting a dead body,
except under very unusual circumstances. Even today,
hospitals are required to obtain permission from next-
of-kin for postmortem examination, an obligation
which antedated our contemporary concern about informed consent. More pertinently, additional consent is
necessary before the skull can be opened and the brain
examined. No other organ needs such special and careful dispensation, as if the equation of brain-mind-soul
were operative. The brain is still sacred territory, and
we are very cautious about trespassing into that domain
where spiritual and mental life is thought to reside.

Another reason for finding the psychological autopsy so paradoxical and repellent is that few people
fully overcome their fear of the dead and dying. Society
has assigned certain professionals to the task of dealing
with death. Doctors are expected to heal people who
are threatened with death; clergymen are to preside
over the passage from this world to whatever else
there is; funeral directors are to arrange suitable
trappings to make the exit less fearsome. These
professionals are subject to mixtures of respect and

ridicule, of awe and anger, to the ambivalences we reserve for anything that reminds us of the margin between life and death.

Regular autopsies have been performed for many generations, but scientific interest in the psychosocial side of death and dying lagged until comparatively recent times. The term "thanatology" was coined by Roswell Park before 1912. Osler devoted much attention to the how and why of dying, as did some of his less famous predecessors and contemporaries. Nevertheless, physicians have continued to believe that their responsibility ends when a patient passes into that limbo of life, called the terminal phase. Nothing more can be done, it is solemnly said, usually in a pious whisper, and the treatment ends. But *when* the terminal phase begins is left ambiguous.

Specialists always talk in strange tongues, especially to each other. The laity likes to hear words that it does not understand. It gives a feeling that these exotic terms are tokens of wisdom and knowledge, and are not far from being magical incantations. From the viewpoint of professionals, they can meet, cluster together, exchange words, nod agreement, but never share viewpoints and ideas. The psychological autopsy method attempts to correct this mutual isolation among health and healing professions. Its common aim is to understand how mankind approaches death. Psychosocial assessment, added to the regular autopsy, aspires to a more comprehensive and comprehensible exchange. The subject is not merely the remains, but the primary person who is thrust forward toward death, whether by illness or intention. Individual feelings, values, responsibilities, relationships—all come under the scrutiny of the psychological autopsy.

LASPC Version

The psychological autopsy procedure was first developed by Shneidman and his associates at the Los Angeles Suicide Prevention Center in the early 1950s. Originally, it was used to investigate the circumstances in which suicide victims sought and found death. The efforts of these pioneers have become the paradigm for other workers in the field of suicidology.

In the LASPC version, a death investigation team was formed. Interviewers went into the community, talked with survivors and significant others, reconstructed the surrounding events of suicide, and then reported back. Theodore Curphey, then the Medical Examiner of Los Angeles County, provided access to case material, and gave freely of his knowledge and experience to the advancement of the method.

Until the LASPC began its investigations, ascribed causes of suicide were, essentially, clichés. Handy phrases—despondency over ill health, family troubles, financial problems, business reverses, history of psychiatric hospitalization—did little to clarify the complexity of suicidal behavior. Oversimplification concealed more than it revealed about suicide.

The LASPC autopsies showed that the distinction between suicidal and nonsuicidal behavior can be tantalizingly uncertain. Certain accidental deaths were found to result from self-destructive behavior, while other deaths, thought to be obvious suicides, turned out to be much more equivocal than expected. Some deaths were neither one nor the other: a victim had placed himself in a precarious situation, participating in his own death without necessarily being overtly suicidal.

Shneidman called these subintentioned deaths, and found still other mixtures of mode and motivation.

The concept of psychological autopsy caught on. Other suicide prevention services reviewed circumstances of death and deadly situations. But it cannot be said that the method gained with its spread and imitation. Agencies vary, as do materials and talent. While the term, psychological autopsy, appeared in writings about suicide, details of the method were lacking. Almost any attempt to reconstruct the history of a suicide was considered by some to be a psychological autopsy.

More recently, Shneidman outlined the information needed for a psychological autopsy (Table 1). He did not, however, specify the details of the procedure, how information is gathered and processed, and what takes place during an autopsy session. Meanwhile, the popularity of the suicidal prevention center concept has waned. Hot lines manned by nonprofessionals have proliferated beyond count. The emphasis has naturally shifted heavily toward community service, and scientific investigation has suffered. Nevertheless, as Allen's monograph on suicide in California demonstrates, the psychological autopsy still has much to offer in the investigation of unexplained death.

Shneidman's outline for the psychological autopsy asks for information about life-style, past history, and presuicidal self-destructive disposition. The material comes from secondary sources, people who knew the victim, not, of course; from the victim himself. This leaves a gap between what others say about a person after a tragic act, and what that person might have said about himself, before and after an attempt. Shneidman has, moreover, always emphasized that a mere outline

Table 1.   Outline for the Psychological Autopsy (LASPC Version)

1. Identifying information for victim (name, age, address, marital status, religious practices, occupation, other details)
2. Details of the death (including cause, method, and other pertinent details)
3. Brief outline of victim's history (siblings, marriage, illnesses, medical treatments, psychiatric treatment, previous attempts)
4. "Death history" of victim's family (suicides, fatal illnesses, ages at death, other details)
5. Personality and life-style of victim
6. Victim's typical reactions to stress, emotional upsets, and periods of disequilibrium
7. Any recent—last few days to 12 months—upsets, pressures, tensions, or anticipation of trouble
8. Role of alcohol and drugs in life-style and in death of victim
9. Victim's relationships with others, including physicians
10. Phantasies, dreams, ideas, premonitions, or fears regarding death, accidents, or suicide
11. Changes in victim before death (habits, hobbies, sexual patterns, life routines)
12. Information relating to "life-side" (upswings, plans, successes)
13. Assessment of intention, i.e., role of victim in his/her own demise
14. Rating of lethality
15. Reaction of informants to victim's death
16. Comments, special features, etc.

Source: E. Shneidman, "Suicide, Lethality, and the Psychological Autopsy," in *Aspects of Depression,* E. Shneidman and M. Ortega (eds.) (Boston: Little, Brown & Co., 1969).

or an accumulation of postmortem data is not an autopsy. The skeleton of information must be fleshed out with the personal responses of each member of the team, so that the psychological autopsy can be a significant occasion. Not only do various team members report, but they participate in a mutual exchange. An evocative atmosphere is difficult to outline, but it offers something more than hard interview schedules, questionnaires, and rating scales.

Anyone who cares enough to find out why another person died or attempted to die wants to be more effective in future dealings with life-threatening situations. Methodology can mask personal anxieties, and a compassionate investigator may use historical data as a shield against too much despair. In almost any hospital or institution where patients come to be cared for by the staff personnel, some version of emotional closure is needed. Unsettled feelings are to be resolved, just as the circumstances of dying and death should be reviewed. Unofficially, sentiments are shared, sometimes even in secret, because to feel something about someone else whom one has known in a professional capacity is often regarded as a transgression.

Most hospitals conduct postmortem examinations in order to be approved or certified. The percentage of autopsies per hospital death is thought to be an index of academic excellence. Staff members are encouraged to obtain and attend autopsies, even where clinico-pathological conferences are not regularly scheduled. However, psychosocial information is glossed over, and the need for open discussion about how the death affected people most concerned is never discussed. As a result, a person who dies as a result of self-injury or poisoning is a subject for description of how organs were damaged and of how normal physiology was compromised. Little is ever said about the erstwhile patient's mental state.

Regular autopsies simply take death as a given fact,

without referring to the subject as a living person. A death investigation team might ask the clinician two salient questions. "Did you expect the patient to die? Why?" To answer these simple questions would be a revolutionary feat. It would expose how little we know about processes of dying, and would also convert the fact of death into a proper area for investigation and assessment. Awareness of the human impact, however, awaits further development of the psychological autopsy. The LASPC version has provided the incentive. Were the full scope of psychosocial factors recognized, no autopsy would be complete without an opportunity for the staff members to share and come to terms with their personal responses. Even in crowded, understaffed city and county hospitals, death is seldom routine.

Geriatric Version

Death investigation is not to be pursued only where death is self-inflicted and untimely, but at the very end of the life cycle, as well. Over a four-year period, Weisman and Kastenbaum conducted weekly sessions at a geriatric hospital, assessing the terminal period of life of over one hundred patients who died. All interested personnel, regardless of professional status, were invited to attend and participate in mutual discussion about a recently deceased patient. No contact, conversation, or observation was regarded as too trivial or incidental to be mentioned.

Although the sessions differed from the LASPC investigations, the conference was called a psychological autopsy. The procedure mirrored the institution itself, and the data reflected the status of patients in a large, state-supported installation. The services in the hospital were largely custodial, although excellent facilities for acute medical and surgical treatment were available. Physiotherapy, occupational and recreational resources were present, but limited personnel kept these services at less than optimum levels. There were case records, but unless a patient had a serious illness, few details were recorded. Notes were irregular; long periods might elapse without an entry. As a result, most of the information volunteered and reported during the autopsy sessions was gleaned from scanty official notes; but spontaneous recollections by relatively untrained staff people, unaccustomed to meeting regularly for any teaching exercise, more than compensated for this deficiency. Psychiatric consultants had been called upon for certain patients through the years, and in a few cases, psychological testing was performed. What was startling, however, was the detailed account of information generated by the group experience itself. People who were largely without systematic training in medical procedures, save, of course, for nurses and an occasional physician, participated enthusiastically. Puzzling situations were clarified by on-the-spot exchanges. Information that was unrecorded and might have been lost was preserved, simply because questions were asked.

The geriatric version of a psychological autopsy developed out of extemporaneous exchange. It was almost the opposite of the LASPC version where trained team members knew what they wanted and had a way of getting it. The geriatric version's format emerged from the fact that many patients had been hospitalized for months and even years. Clinical stages therefore were divided into phases called the *prehospital situa-tion, hospital course, preterminal period,* and *final illness* (Table 2).

Patients did not customarily receive close attention unless they developed acute physical symptoms, such as heart failure, cerebral thromboses and hemorrhages, respiratory infections, or injuries. Because family members might visit more frequently at these times, psychosocial observations then were likely to be re-corded. If the patient became very ill, requiring inten-sive treatment, then much more information was avail-able. Little was known about the prehospital situation. Social workers briefly interviewed a relative, but their conversations were apt to be confined to financial and physical disabilities. Slightly more was known about the hospital course. Visitors might come and go, or not appear at all. Events were occasionally recorded, such as the death of a close relative, a leave of absence, or an administrative problem.

It seemed to the investigators that the geriatric psychological autopsy was like an archaeological dig. The recent past and final illness offered much informa-tion. As they tried to reconstruct the past, however, facts became sparse and scanty. Only a fragment from the remoter periods, i.e., prehospital situation (which, after all, comprised most of the patients' lives), could be found here and there. Nevertheless, in the absence of facts, artifacts were found—an incident occurring years before, a notebook found in a bedstand, an unusual bit of behavior, a phrase repeated over and over, an argu-ment, an anniversary, even an injury. Some of these fragments prompted one of the attending participants to recall something else, which in turn stimulated others to remember. And in surprising ways, recollec-

Table 2. Outline for the Psychological Autopsy
(Geriatric Version)

I. *Final Illness*
   1. What was the patient's terminal illness?
   2. Did this illness differ substantially from admission diagnoses?
   3. Was the death expected or unexpected at this time? Why?
   4. Was death sudden or gradual?
   5. Was autopsy permission granted? By whom?

II. *Preterminal Period*
   1. What was the mental status and level of consciousness prior to the terminal illness?
   2. What drew attention to mental, physical, or social changes?
   3. What references did the patient make to death, dying, or decline?
   4. Were there any indirect indications of impending death?
   5. What were the patient's relationships during this period?

III. *Hospital Course*
   1. What were the extent and nature of patient's relationships—staff, other patients, family, visitors, etc.—during the overall course?
   2. How was the patient regarded by those in closest contact?
   3. What personal problems or crises developed, and how were they met?

IV. *Prehospital Situation*
   1. What was the patient's medical and mental status at the time of admission?
   2. What medical, social, and personal circumstances led to hospitalization?
   3. What was the patient's attitude toward admission?

Source: A. Weisman and R. Kastenbaum, *The Psychological Autopsy: A Study of the Terminal Phase of Life,* Community Mental Health Monograph, No. 4 (New York: Behavioral Publications, 1968).

tions, surmises, and reconstructions fitted together, enabling the investigators to infer something about how the patient under discussion regarded death and dying.

The lesson learned was emphatically clear. Even the most unpromising records and casual contacts, coupled with intensified care during acute or terminal illness, can tell a great deal, especially in the setting of group interactions.

One example illustrates the method. A few days before an elderly patient died, an attendant decided to clean out the junk in the bedside stand. What was the junk? Oh, only a few scraps of paper, a snapshot or two, postcards from years back, some dates written down. Each of these items evoked a response from another participant. Yes, the patient had kept snapshots of her children, whom she had not seen in several years. The dates? No one knew for sure. Birthdays? Anniversaries? The postcards were from her husband, who died within the past year, and from someone else, identified by a first name only. We could not be sure, without undertaking an impracticable investigation what all this signified, except that the so-called junk was all that linked the patient to her past. These were treasures, not junk. So we must assume that to be deprived of mementos, without consent, led to withdrawal (which was confirmed), physical decline, and death.

Through similar examples, as well as more conventional reports and retorts, we learned how to scan sketchy but provocative incidents. Spontaneous comments were not always very illuminating, but the extemporaneous interchange sometimes brought out highly personal disclosures about grief and anger that no other method could have elicited. The experience gained under these unpromising circumstances led to the principle of *guided selectivity* in monitoring more ample information later on, when the psychological autopsy was used in a general hospital.

Omega Version

The rest of this discussion concerns the psychological autopsy method as adapted and applied in a large general hospital, where records are more complete, the staff is highly trained, and information more profuse, if not always pertinent to the task of clarifying death and dying.

The Omega version differs from the LASPC and geriatric versions in four important respects: (1) actual contact with the patient, usually for days or weeks, (2) detailed past history, both from the patient and from hospital records, (3) interviews with significant others and with primary staff members, and (4) multidisciplinary assessments during hospitalization.

While the autopsy itself consists of retrospective reconstruction, the original data come from direct and sometimes lengthy interviews with the primary person, the patient, from families and friends, before and often after the demise, and from professionals who had known and taken care of the patient on previous admissions.

In cases of suicide attempts, we have psychiatric information from other sources, including that of hospital records of illness and other injuries. Operative notes, laboratory tests, social service reports, and nursing records are available. For the first time, therefore, the

psychological autopsy method could call upon trained
observers to gather information over a longer period,
and then to meet regularly, exchanging views, confirming and dissenting. Above all, the more information
available for assessment, the more conspicuous become
the questions still to be asked.

Comparison with the Regular Autopsy

Before proceeding to how the psychological autopsy works, it is well to review how it differs and
complements the regular autopsy. The psychological
autopsy has far to go. It needs generations of practice
and application under different circumstances, using
other instruments for collecting data, fresh concepts,
and many other considerations, as yet undefined.

The regular autopsy deserves its prestige; its history is the record of how rationality triumphs over
superstition—and is sometimes spurred by the compla-
cent ignorance of preconceptions. Even allowing for its
novelty, the psychological autopsy can scarcely be
compared with the regular autopsy. The regular
autopsy—it should be called the necropsy—has a dead
body to dissect, with organs to examine and analyze,
according to principles and procedures established
elsewhere, in hospitals, laboratories, and experimental
stations. There are instruments of precision, such as the
microscope, sensitive tests for chemical and physiological abnormalities, and abundantly cross-indexed, stan-
dard nomenclatures.

Although anatomical lesions do not always corre-
late well with clinical aberrations, there is sufficient

knowledge to indicate probable causes of death in most cases. In contrast, the psychological autopsy searches for the context of death, not its causes. For example, a patient may yearn for death during a serious illness —and then promptly recover. Even very stressful and deleterious events do not necessarily culminate in death. There are no outer limits of despair and misery that are not compatible with human endurance and survival. People can die of poverty, brutalization, demoralization, and suffering, but not until starvation, infection, or fatal injuries finally compromise physical functions.

The intervening variables between psychosocial stress and physical death are unknown, with methods now available. Therefore, the psychological autopsy, as presently conceived, does not tell us why someone died when he did. Rather, it examines the events, social, personal, and physical, leading away from the moment of death, evaluating and often reassessing what happened on the way to death. Many factors, briefly noted, may turn out to be highly significant in retrospect. Yet other events, obviously death-related, may have only a cumulative effect, but without physical correlates.

The psychological autopsy does not, therefore, need a dead body; the focal event which is the occasion of an autopsy can be drawn from any kind of death-related situation or life-threatening behavior—the scope of thanatology. The threat of death or one of its secondary signs is a sufficient reason to examine antecedents. Another term could be used, but because of Shneidman's work and the inspiration of the autopsy procedure itself, I prefer to use the original name for this type of enterprise.

How does the psychological autopsy differ from the ordinary case conference in psychiatry? Why work out a special procedure for death and dying? Are psychiatrists necessary? In the first place, the psychological autopsy is not primarily a psychiatric exercise. Our concern, regardless of professional vocation, is with the human predicament, not with psychopathology, a curious discipline at best. Our specific concern is that part of the human predicament which might result in death. Therefore, while we are naturally alert to aberrations of thought, emotion, and behavior, the patient studied need not have shown overt psychiatric symptoms or disorders.

Death is a psychosomatic event, but systematic appraisals of death and dying, even discussions about death-related situations, are almost as alien to ordinary case conferences in psychiatry as to regular autopsies. The psychiatrist is not an indispensable member of the psychological autopsy team. Obviously, a psychiatrist should have facility to interview patients about psychosocial topics, and someone with these skills is also likely to be a qualified psychiatrist. But the essence of the autopsy is not psychiatric, as presently understood. Any specialist in human behavior could coordinate serious studies of how people respond on the threshold of death. Most suicidologists, for example, are not psychiatrists, nor even physicians. The psychological autopsy needs various specialists, as our core staff exemplified, including the equivalent of a "pathologist" to preside over the discussion and to draw different data together.

Chapter 3

PROCEDURES

What Do We Look For?

The value of what is observed depends more upon a patient's personal concerns than upon mere accumulation of medical and nursing notes. Procedure can be divided according to three questions: What do we want to do? How is it done? How can we tell if we did it?

Most patients are primarily concerned about their health and physical problems—what is wrong, what can be done, and who will treat them. Beyond this, however, patients with chronic illness or with serious illness that disrupts their ordinary course of activities have problems about work, family, finances, self-esteem, religious concerns, and existential issues, especially if their life is threatened.

It would be impossible to categorize every human concern, much less to compile a list of specific conflicts and crises that would, like a signature, identify every patient. The psychological autopsy method uses a limited number of general topics which can be defined readily and constitute what is looked for:

1. Focal events
2. Precursors and precipitants
3. Significant key others and other kinds of support
4. Key decisions, diagnoses, aims, treatments
5. Psychosocial stages
6. Retrospective assessments

Focal Events

The reason for the autopsy is called a focal event. It may be an actual death, but more often it is a recent death-related occasion—a suicide attempt, serious operation, life and death crisis, terminal illness, or the like. Because most psychological autopsies investigate hospitalized patients, the focal event has four components: (1) final or most immediate physical illness, injury, or death related episode, (2) hospital behavior, (3) personal responses of the patient during the focal period, and (4) general social origin, context of relationships, and interpersonal events during the recent past. These four parts are avenues by which different investigators can approach the focal event—the physician, psychiatrist, psychologist, nurse-clinician, and social worker. There is overlapping by design, but separation by discipline. The focal event is agreed upon, and then, regardless of the avenue used, becomes the index for all investigation and discussion.

Precursors and Precipitants

Any focal event is surrounded by a variety of episodes, events, and transactions. Some are wholly incidental; others have equivocal relevance; a few seem to have compelling significance. The presumption of relevance between an antecedent event and the focal event may not be decided until much later. But we note every occurrence that just might turn out to be critical. These initial events are called precursors simply because they precede the focal event. For example, an elderly woman was hospitalized for terminal cancer. During hospitalization, her daughter was suddenly stricken with abdominal pain, and taken to a local hospital. The son-in-law had to stay out of work to care for his children. The focal event in this case turned out to be the patient's later demise. But the initial precursor was the daughter's hospitalization. At the moment of learning about her daughter, the patient began to weep, worrying inordinately about her grandchildren and feeling very remiss for not being at home. Note that the daughter went to the hospital after her mother's hospitalization, so that we cannot hold that one event precipitated the other. Because our patient died within a short time, still believing that her place was at home, the precursor of death and possibly one among many other precipitants was the hospitalization-depression. A precipitant is a precursor whose connection with the focal event is established. In retrospect, we judged that the hospitalization of the daughter precipitated self-reproach and depression, although the patient had suffered from cancer for several years and might have died before long anyway.

The distinction between precursors and precipitants is not academic. We do not attempt to assign causal meaning to these events, but to identify related events within an active psychosocial field. In the previous chapter, it was presumed during the geriatric autopsy that throwing away the junk in a patient's bedside table was not only a precursor but a precipitant of the patient's subsequent decline. In another example, an aged widow lost her pet parakeet shortly before being hospitalized for a cerebrovascular disorder. She was saddened by the bird's death, but referred to the event only in passing, during an interview. Shall the parakeet's death be considered a precursor, which it is, or a genuine precipitant? The question cannot be answered with dogmatic certainty. But if the pet's death evoked a degree of depression and loneliness, which often happens with aged people living alone, it is likely that loss of the parakeet was a precipitant. Obviously, enthusiasm can label many events, but only a few are termed precipitants, because we must look for the emotional impact and social disruption that a precursor produces before stating that one event precipitates another.

Significant Key Others and Other Kinds of Support

Someone with whom a patient has had a sustaining and mutual relationship is called a significant key other (SKO). Formal kinship relations with spouses, siblings, offspring, parents, and inlaws are not necessarily those of an SKO, because the nature of the relationship has not been identified as one which has critical significance. Mutuality and intimacy are better criteria for "key" others than are family relations, as such. Key relationships need not be unambivalently supportive; there are many love/hate situations in which neither person can get along with or without the other. Good friends may move away, or die. SKOs may not be able to tolerate the misfortunes surrounding a fatal illness. In cases of suicide attemptors, the significant other may die, lose interest, turn to someone else, or betray trust in some other way.

Family members are always asked about, even if they are not close to the patient. The number and age of others at death, as well as the causes of death, sometimes show inexplicable connections. Project Omega has several examples of families in whom tragedy seems to strike at special times of the year. It is not unusual to learn that a patient with a fatal illness also lost his parents at the same age.

Significant key others are listed in order of importance to the patient's current equilibrium and living arrangements. A common question asked is, "Whom would you miss most, if they weren't around for any reason?"

People may choose to live alone, or be forced to do so by necessity. Few are so isolated or self-sufficient that they have no wish for friends, family, or sustaining, supportive activities. SKOs are not always present; other kinds of support (OKS), such as hobbies, pets, work, community projects, recreational interests, church activities, may be significant forces in a person's social-emotional field, enabling him to maintain a balance between stress and satisfaction. Changes in these supports, like losses of SKOs, may precipitate disequilibrium and perhaps also decline.

We should also recognize that during a terminal illness, or during any stressful period of hospitalization, significant others may be the professionals. The patient-doctor relation needs no further emphasis, but

there are relationships between nursing staff and patient, or between social worker and family, that go
beyond narrow considerations of physical well-being.
There are realistic relations which develop, as well as
difficult transferences and countertransferences. If a
significant professional is lost, or seems to become
discouraged or angry, it is apt to undermine whatever
precarious hold a patient has on the rest of the world.
Suicidal patients, for example, are particularly vulnerable to their doctor's absence, even construing normal
vacations as abandonment. This observation could almost certainly be repeated for any other significant
professional relation.

Key Decisions, Diagnoses, Aims, and Treatments

Sometimes it seems that how a decision is arrived
at matters more than the decision itself. As noted
before, diagnosis is not simply a rubric of classification
but a series of activities and a plan of management.
There are many other decisions made with and about a
patient which scarcely ever are made explicit. For
example, a decision to move a patient from one room to
another for administrative reasons may unwittingly
change the surrounding psychosocial field. As a result, a
cooperative patient may become antagonistic, depressed, fearful, and isolated. As Omega observers visit
various wards, it is often significant to notice where a
patient has been placed. Patients in whom the nursing
staff is interested are usually near the nursing station,
while other patients can be "exiled" to a room at the far
end of the corridor. Interactions go on all the time, of

course. What is said, how it is said, and when it is said deserve careful examination, and should not be accepted at face value. There is a conspicuous difference between what one means to say, and what one is heard to say. As a rule, what is said and done reflect a policy about patient care. And some policies are individually oriented, while others are simply designed to carry out ward work expeditiously.

Decisions are made whenever someone recognizes a problem, and tries to cope with it. Many of these problems concern how a patient is to be treated, both as a person and as a victim of an illness. Suicide attemptors may be regarded with disdain by some staff members. Their dedication to saving lives does not dispose them to accepting someone who, on the surface, has deliberately put his life in jeopardy. Certain doctors tend to withhold medication from terminal patients, expecting that survival will be long enough for addiction to be a serious problem. Key decisions of this kind are apt to make a patient hesitate before complaining, lest he offend or alienate the people on whom he depends. As life comes to a close, doctors may choose to administer drugs and treatment which are tokens of treatment, without expecting any beneficial effect. The aim is palliation, but is also designed to keep the doctors from feeling as helpless as they are. In doing so, regardless of the merits, certain expectations and concerns are conveyed along with various ministrations. Patients have their own expectations about illness, then about their treatment, then about their refractoriness to treatment, and finally about the professionals with whom they have entrusted their care. Conversely, every hospital, like every individual, lives by certain rules, directives, and prohibitions. There are codes of behavior which patients are expected to obey in order to be considered "good patients." Even opinions about prognosis and aims are colored by rules and expectations. Not infrequently, choice of management, which comes from a prognostic opinion, is decided as much by whether a patient is likable than absolutely scientific criteria.

Investigators who have the psychological autopsy in mind do not necessarily confine themselves to patients who will die. The psychological autopsy is simply a method of collecting data and recognizing certain preexisting problems. Consequently, observers are alert to how staff members express themselves about patients. Even a twist of phrase or a manner of speaking can reveal a great deal about the professional relationship. The Omega observer uses direct interrogation and indirect inferences from diverse facts. We can ask a doctor or nurse how they like a certain patient. Since it is not often that a professional will express open dislike, we can be more circumspect, asking what a patient might do to help himself more. Recall the two "revolutionary" questions: "Did you expect the patient to die? Why?"

Psychosocial Stages

The psychosocial evaluation considers what has happened to a patient over time, beginning with the prediagnostic period, then the intermediate interval of established disease, and finally, the stage of deterioration, decline, and death. Psychosocial stages are primarily *time intervals* in which different events occur along with changes in anatomical and clinical status. There are three principal psychosocial stages. *Stage 1* is the prediagnostic and diagnostic period. It starts with the first symptoms or signs and ends with the definitive diagnosis. During this time interval, patients may delay with or without denial, or presume themselves to be seriously ill, yet postpone seeking help. Some say, "It's nothing"; others will ask, immediately, "What is it?" Still others postpone on one pretext or another, "Right after Christmas . . . when my son graduates . . . too busy . . . I'm afraid of the doctor . . . and what he might say." *Stage 2* is the period of established disease. During this time, a patient is under care or at least under periodic observation and treatment. Psychosocial problems can be documented, even though they are not necessarily products of concomitant physical changes. *Stage 3* signals deterioration, decline, failure to respond, new symptoms, complications and side effects of drugs, then dying. There is no sharp line to mark the end of stage 2 and the start of stage 3. Aside from telltale anatomical and clinical signs of decline, the people affiliated with the patient may themselves decide that terminality is approaching. Their behavior changes, and expectations also change. The sequence of special stages in fatal illness should be correlated with events involving the dimensions of death—impersonal, interpersonal, and intrapersonal. In other words, the observer notes organic and personal perspectives and places the person into a setting in which every detectable influential occurrence can be recorded. An even simpler staging process says that a patient is first sick, then becomes sicker, then very sick, and finally the sickest of all.

Table 3.　Psychosocial Stages of Fatal Illness

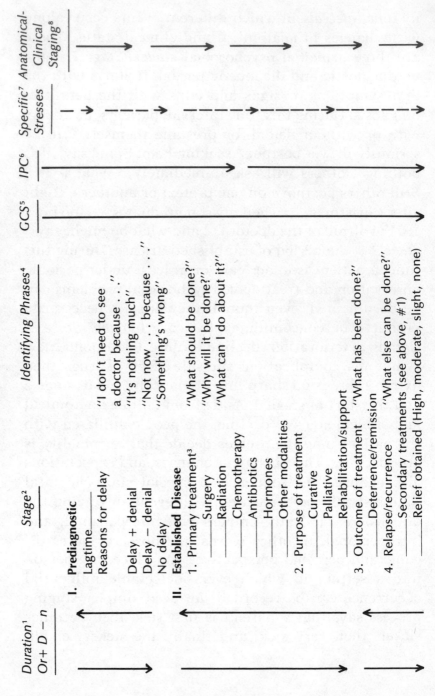

Duration[1] Or+ D − n	Stage[2]	Identifying Phrases[4]	GCS[5]	IPC[6]	Specific[7] Stresses	Anatomical-Clinical Staging[8]
	I.　Prediagnostic					
	Lagtime					
	Reasons for delay	"I don't need to see a doctor because . . ." "It's nothing much"				
	Delay + denial	"Not now . . . because . . ."				
	Delay − denial	"Something's wrong"				
	No delay					
	II.　Established Disease					
	1. Primary treatment[3]	"What should be done?"				
	——Surgery	"Why will it be done?"				
	——Radiation	"What can I do about it?"				
	——Chemotherapy					
	——Antibiotics					
	——Hormones					
	——Other modalities					
	2. Purpose of treatment					
	——Curative					
	——Palliative					
	——Rehabilitation/support					
	3. Outcome of treatment	"What has been done?"				
	——Deterrence/remission					
	4. Relapse/recurrence	"What else can be done?"				
	——Secondary treatments (see above, #1)					
	——Relief obtained (High, moderate, slight, none)					

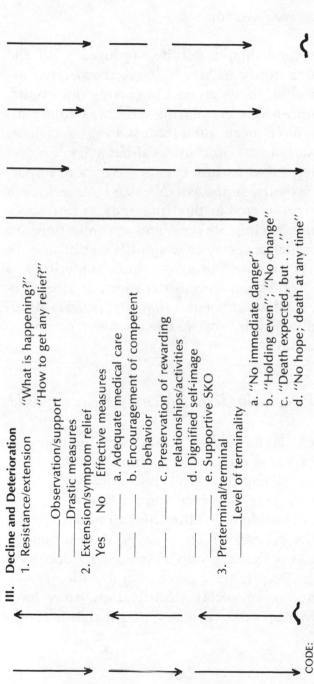

III. Decline and Deterioration

1. Resistance/extension   "What is happening?"
                            "How to get any relief?"

   ____ Observation/support
        Drastic measures

2. Extension/symptom relief

   Yes   No   Effective measures

   ____ ____ a. Adequate medical care
   ____ ____ b. Encouragement of competent
                   behavior
   ____ ____ c. Preservation of rewarding
                   relationships/activities
   ____ ____ d. Dignified self-image
   ____ ____ e. Supportive SKO

3. Preterminal/terminal

   ____ Level of terminality

        a. "No immediate danger"
        b. "Holding even"; "No change"
        c. "Death expected, but . . ."
        d. "No hope; death at any time"

CODE:

1. *Duration.* Or+ = time from original complaint. D − n = time from death.
2. *Stage.* See text for definition of stages. Lagtime = from first symptom until any doctor is seen. Delay = lagtime plus additional time due to misdiagnosis/observation by original doctor.
3. *Primary treatment.* Period of established disease is defined according to treatment and the patient's response within the psychosocial setting.
4. *Identifying phrases.* These are typical comments at different stages which serve identifying functions.
5. *GCS.* See Table 4, General Coping Strategies.
6. *IPC.* Inventory of Predominant Concerns, e.g., Health, Family/friends, Work/finances, Self-appraisal, Religion, Mood/mental status, Existential/time perspective.
7. *Specific stresses.* These are significant external events. See text, Precursors/precipitants.
8. *Anatomical-clinical staging.* Anatomical = I—Local; II—Regional; III—Distant. Clinical = I—Local; II—Systemic; III— Disseminated.

Retrospective Assessments

This category should not be confused with the psychological autopsy as a whole. Retrospective assessment is a continuous process of sorting out events, correcting impressions, comparing what was done with what might have been done, evaluating decisions, treatments, statements, and interval-behavior. Second sight may reveal that certain events were more important than originally supposed. A casual remark or a question, scarcely noted at the time, may in retrospect have a prophetic ring. Review and reevaluation are necessary in order properly to weigh the significance of events. This is an inner process which sometimes is simply called reflection, reconsideration, and reworking. The name is less important than the process itself, an example of which is how we can change a precursor into a precipitant.

How Is a Psychological Autopsy Conducted?

Teamwork is far easier to talk about than to achieve. The term is often used to smooth over differences between disciplines. Not infrequently, it is a pleasantry signifying not very much. Genuine teamwork requires considerable effort and time before friction can be overcome, which it never is, completely. Teamwork means that a group of specialists decide to work together. Despite their professional pride, jargon, sensitivity, and even social stratification, they have enough confidence, skill, curiosity, and insight to compromise.

Many so-called teams are committees in which some members carry more weight and authority than do others. As the cases in the following chapter illustrate, our group retained much of the committee system, despite efforts to diminish the pyramid of authority and influence. Two prominent hazards of teamwork are exposed during the process of evaluating and sharing an endeavor. These hazards are *conflict* and *consensus*. Neither will be strongly apparent in the condensed case reports. One person's perception may be another person's error. There are conflicts between personalities as well as between disciplines. Honest differences of opinion are to be encouraged, but we have found conflict in participants who debate the significance of almost every observation. Some Omega observers, a phrase used to indicate anyone who has a professional interest in the phenomena related to death, become preoccupied with details, and tenaciously struggle with minutiae. Others favor the free-flowing conjecture, unhampered by data. Both extremes can obstruct the spontaneity of the group. Consensus is a hazard indigenous to people who work together. Like people who live together, they sometimes tend to think alike, expecting certain things to happen, and as a result, they implicitly ignore the exceptions, novelties, or breaches of rules they have set up for themselves.

Our procedures for conducting a psychological autopsy are not prototypes, but guides. Other observers who work in different kinds of institutions will, almost certainly, perform autopsies in accordance with prevailing circumstances and material.

Core Staff

The core staff of Project Omega consisted of psychiatrists, psychologists, a social worker, and a nurse-clinician. It would have been helpful had a member of the medical or surgical staff regularly participated. Chaplains also have a special role, and could well become a functioning member of any core staff.

Patients respond differently from one observer to another. This indubitable fact can be attributed as much to the interviewer's personality as to his methods of assessment. The time of an interview (e.g., morning or evening), place (on the ward or in a private room), manner, and professional role have an influence on a patient's demeanor and disclosure. Moreover, there is an indefinable chemistry between people which sparks one relationship and dulls another. Different observations may result.

Naturally, interested visitors are encouraged, but only if they can actively participate in the group process, either through an acquaintance with the patient under discussion or because of special knowledge of a related subject. Too many participants spoil the interchange, just as in group therapy. However, a visitor who can contribute a story, recall a conversation, or even relate an encounter with the patient's friends or family, will be a valuable addition.

Format

Logistics are simple. The autopsy starts with an initial statement, followed by individual reports. Then there is a pause for further questions and clarifications. Psychological test results are then given, after which the group discusses salient issues, which are summarized by the chairman who has guided the session. Ordinarily, time spent for a psychological autopsy is about two hours, never more.

The chairman (yes, like a committee) presides, but his function is like a pathologist at a regular autopsy. He initiates the session by briefly stating the presenting problem, calls on participants, asks questions, and summarizes the material at the end.

The social worker usually reports first. His contact with significant others establishes a baseline assessment of what the patient was like before hospitalization. Social, economic, occupational, family, community, and other types of relationships and categories provide background information. The social worker also maintains contact after hospitalization or transfer. He checks on physical status, and even on bereavement responses in the family.

The psychiatrist is next to report. He emphasizes interviews with the patient, focusing on predominant concerns, coping strategies, defenses, conflicts, mood, mental status, key hospital events, and signs of vulnerability. To stimulate further exchanges, the psychiatrist is urged to disclose his own personal responses. Not only does this permit better clarification; it helps the rest of the core staff to recognize possible distortions and artifacts.

Logically, a staff physician should report at this juncture. The physician with primary responsibility for the patient would tell about physical changes and treatments. He might also be questioned about the reasons for the decisions he made during the illness. As a substitute for the primary physician, the head nurse on the patient's floor often presents her views about general behavior, response to treatment, and range of reactions. The hospital record itself is read in advance of the meeting, and pertinent members of the staff have been interviewed. A summary of these findings is presented by the psychiatrist, usually before interviews with the patient are reported.

The nurse-clinician has daily contact with patients. Consequently, if a patient dies or is transferred to another institution, or is merely discharged, she has a detailed, running account to report. She has also interviewed members of the nursing staff who have more extensive observations than are likely to be recorded.

After these preliminary reports from the core staff, there is an interval for asking questions. The pause is deliberate for several reasons. As a rule, a report is very condensed and needs elaboration. Furthermore, after the pause, the psychologist will present test results. If reports are all run together, they tend to fuse and confuse. Controversial points may be skipped over. Participants also revise their reports in the light of psychological tests, apparently believing that test instruments are less fallible and more objective than clinical observations.

Many psychological tests are available. We have found it practical to use a basic battery consisting of a modified Thematic Apperception Test (TAT), Profile of Mood States (POMS), a Sentence Completion Test devised for our special needs, and the Cole Animal Test. In brain damage cases, other tests have been used. One of the major problems in longitudinal studies is how to handle vast amounts of information in a systematic way. We have developed several inventories called, at present, the Index of Vulnerability, General Coping Strategies, Predominant Concerns, and an Effectiveness Profile. These instruments were not used during Omega I but have proved to be exceedingly helpful during Omega II. While it is unnecessary to describe each of these instruments for the purposes of the psychological autopsy, several of our forms are shown in the Appendix.

Omega Chronology

The chronology of sickness usually starts with the first symptoms and ends—for our purposes –with the focal event. The psychological autopsy reverses the sequence, starting with the focal event and retrospectively dating episodes from that point. For example, if the focal event is a patient's death, omega chronology would be $D-n$, where D =death and n =number of days, weeks, or months at which a specific event occurred. Thus, we can be more accurate in locating an event, both from the onset of illness and from the focal event. Observers can compare findings more precisely, and discrepancies can be more readily explained. For instance, one report may be dated on the $D-3$ day, while another is based on the $D-1$ day. Both pertain to 72 hours before death, but the value of omega chronology is that, within that time, the patient could have been moved to another room, given a new medication, and had unexpected visitors on the $D-2$ day which changed things around. Much disputation about who is right and why certain behavior takes place when it does can be eliminated by dating events according to the omega chronology.

Retrospective Questions

Discussion seldom waits for each report to be completed. Others interrupt, go off on tangents, anticipate their own comments, and raise highly pertinent questions that time prevents answering. The chairman must exercise *guided selectivity* both to choose topics for discussion and to control the course of the autopsy. Since not every question or procedure can be undertaken with limited time at our disposal, at the end of the session certain remaining issues can be opened up. Typical retrospective questions are:

1. What medical, social, and personal precursors seemed to precipitate the focal event?
2. When did the preterminal (or presuicidal) period begin?
3. What were the premonitory signs of imminent death?
4. How did this patient tend to cope with concerns from time to time?
5. To what extent was this patient aware of fatal illness?
6. How much actual control could this patient keep over outside events, over his medication, or over relationships?
7. Knowing what we now do, how could psychosocial factors have been managed differently? What might we do over?

8. To what extent did the focal event resolve remaining problems?
9. What else do we still want to know? Can we find out?
10. What has this case taught us about death that we didn't know before?

Premortem Interviewing

The principles of interviewing suicidal and fatally ill patients have been discussed elsewhere, and do not properly belong in a book about the psychological autopsy. Nevertheless, the psychological autopsy depends upon adequate premortem information, regardless of healthy improvisation and spontaneous interchanges.

The basic prerequisite for interviewing is to be found in the person of the interviewer. How the interviewer tolerates the threat of death modifies the inquiry. Like almost everyone else, patients are usually willing to talk about themselves and their illness. Given ample time and compassion, even forbearance, interviewers can be very supportive and still get much information.

It is very easy for an interviewer to set up a data base by asking preformed questions in a stereotyped way. But the interview is not simply designed to get information; it is a method of assessment, and the interviewer is an instrument of assessment, as well. Instruments need constant monitoring and adjustment: preconceptions, resistance, and personal emotions influence how readily an interviewer perceives and adjusts himself to various nuances. Unrecognized interactions will even alter the nature of the material which is elicited.

Interviews with patients who face death will have a mutual impact. Few people completely overcome their death fears. To bring out individual information suitable for reporting to one's colleagues and at the same time offering support is an art, skill, and talent which, nevertheless, can be learned, practiced, and taught to others.

Medical information is impersonal, and can be obtained without much personal involvement. However, psychosocial data cannot be isolated from the person giving information and from the person asking for information. We inquire gently and compassionately. Tact is uppermost but we do not back off when certain data are required. We avoid yes/no questions. We pose open-ended inquiries which invite elaboration, but do not interrogate. At the very beginning, an effective interviewer often imagines what a patient was like before he first became ill. Then the changes that illness and failure to recover induce can be kept in perspective.

Generations of physicians have asked the timeworn question, "How do you feel?" This can be just another trite inquiry, which asks only for a noncommittal answer: "OK," "No good," "Fine." But the same question, asked by someone who is genuinely concerned—"*How* do you feel?", How *do* you feel?", "How do *you* feel?", or "How do you *feel*?"—may elicit four different responses, each of which may be followed by other inquiries.

In interviewing fatally ill or suicidal patients, we are not merely collecting impersonal information, but attempting to find out how someone else construes the world. Our questions are couched in familiar language which moves readily in response to various clues and cues. Even the most casual question can be informative. The most relaxed approach can be alert. The most flexible interviewing style may turn out to be the most comprehensive. For example, the following questions, taken from an initial interview schedule for use with recently diagnosed cancer patients, are typical:

1. How did you happen to see the doctor and come to the hospital at this time?
2. Who suggested that you come? How undecided were *you*?
3. In your opinion, what might have brought on this condition? What did you think when it first developed?
4. Right now, what bothers you most of all? How does this condition make a difference in the people you're closest to? What have you said to them, if anything?
5. As a rule, whom do you depend on most . . . like to be with . . . trust?
6. What do you usually do when you're feeling down . . . angry . . . afraid? What happens when you don't get your own way?
7. When someone you really cared about went away, say, in the past—for any reason—how did you feel? What could make you feel like that again now?
8. As you look back over the past few years, what are some things you really feel good about? What about the things that didn't turn out well, disappointed you, caused some heartache or

regrets? Whose fault was it? If you had it to do over, what would you do differently?

9. What would you see yourself doing, say, a year from now? What could interfere, if anything?
10. Tell me, at this very moment, what do you think about your entire situation?

Note that in a very short span, these few all-purpose questions open up and survey the personal past, present plight, anticipated future, physical symptoms, disabilities, regrets, problem areas, salient concerns, coping strategies, and signs of psychosocial vulnerability. These questions can be asked in any order. Responses are easily recorded, even rated, according to our estimation of their importance for future inquiry. Using this base of information, we can venture into specific topics before returning to the original questions. The flow of material and the tide of the interview determine its progress. But there is no rule, phraseology, or format applying to every patient and every contingency.

Patience and tact can be learned. Seemingly unimportant details such as taking time to sit down and to establish eye-to-eye contact can be extremely decisive, separating the perfunctory technician from the concerned participant. We seek to reduce the disparity between a healthy, vertical interviewer and an ill, horizontal patient. Data will assuredly emerge; existential contact is what we want.

To discover how a patient generally copes, we can ask what he or she does when something goes wrong . . . doesn't get his or her own way . . . and so forth. Then we ask, "What did you do (are doing) about it?", "How did it work out?", "What do you think others might do (or have done)?", and "Would you do the same again?"

Not every patient responds in the same way. They differ as to cooperation as well as in capacity to understand and to articulate. The same patient may vary from time to time, even with the same interviewer. He may be too sick or sedated, or be beyond caring. Still we must reach out in appropriate ways, allowing for regression, reticence, resentment, and denial. In any event, most patients need the assurance that the person asking questions will return, and, if needed further, will be there. Regardless of professional specialty, we look for authentic and accurate information. The psychological autopsy has few tests for reliability. We must therefore develop our skills and sensitivities. This comes about through reading, consultation with others, supervision, exchange of ideas, testing out alternative procedures, but most of all, by openness to new and revealing experiences.

Chapter 4
CASE ILLUSTRATIONS

Although over a hundred psychological autopsies were recorded, transcriptions of conferences are more apt to stultify than to stimulate the imagination. Reading the proceedings of any meeting in which several people participate is one of the most tedious exercises yet devised by man. In choosing cases to illustrate the types of problems that the psychological autopsy deals with, I have had three guides. Is the case representative? Can it be condensed? Will confidentiality be preserved? The latter consideration is of utmost importance. Without assurance that the privacy of patients and families can be adequately protected, there would be no point in recommending that the method be used. Consequently, certain facts, events, and places have been changed, and, of course, the names used are fictitious. In so proceeding, the central problem that the case illustrated also had to be preserved. When self-imposed censorship required too many changes, simply to present the problem, the case was dropped, and several intriguing autopsies were lost in this way. No special permission for publication was required. Patients and families cooperated in the investigation, simply as hospitalized patients. They were interviewed and followed just as other patients and families would be. As will be seen, families cooperated and failed to cooperate, just as other families do.

The problem of condensability was solved by drastic, if not Draconian measures. Each autopsy is presented as succinctly as possible. In order to condense the reports, give-and-take interchanges, ripostes, and digressions that enliven any meeting are all but gone. As a result, some of the case illustrations will seem quite stilted and rehearsed. Others will be like any case conference that dwindles into uncertainty as time runs out. A modest amount of explanation has been inserted to clarify certain typical issues and problems, but the expository parts should not be considered definitive reviews of the literature or the last word on any subject. As much as possible, I have simultaneously shortened case discussions and underscored salient topics, while trying to preserve some of the spirit of a psychological autopsy. Occasional references are for the reader's convenience only; they were not part of the original session.

In the process of revising transcripts, an artifact was created. Active staff members may seem not to contribute very much, aside from asking an occasional question. This was not true in general, nor even for particular cases. Although not everyone participated to the same extent, there was usually a high level of

exchange. Instead of using names, the following ab-
breviations refer to members of the core staff:

ADW—Avery D. Weisman, M.D.
FGG—Frederick G. Guggenheim, M.D.
HSO—Harry S. Olin, M.D.
JWW—J. William Worden, Ph.D.
JPL—Joe P. Lemon, M.S.W.
RSS—Robert Sterling-Smith, Ph.D.
LCJ—Lee C. Johnston, Ph.D.
MLV—Mary L. Vallier, R.N., M.A.

Occasional visitors are indicated by the initials, IP, for
"invited participant." While we appreciate deeply their
interest and contributions, identification of spoken remarks was not considered necessary.

Case 1. Precursors of Death

ADW

The case for today was a sixty-six-year-old housewife who died of Hodgkin's Disease (Stage IV, B) about
one year after the diagnosis.

Her main symptoms were fatigue, fever, and dysp-
nea. There was minimal pain throughout the course of
illness, and she was alert and coherent almost until the
moment of death.

We established omega contact about six months
before she died. Four months before death she was
transferred to a chronic care hospital. It was there that
she died. Our staff saw her only occasionally after

transfer, so we are glad to welcome the social workers who saw the patient during intervals between hospitalizations, and then after admission to the chronic hospital.

I hope that we will concentrate upon the psychological precursors—intrapersonal and interpersonal—that characterized the patient's illness and death.

Let us first hear about the patient's background.

JPL

This lady had two living children. There was a married daughter, aged twenty-eight, and an unmarried son, aged twenty-three. The son caused the patient much trouble, starting in his boyhood with truancy and car thefts to his adulthood. He was a drug pusher and user of hard drugs. After getting a dishonorable army discharge, he shuttled between jail and home, drinking to excess, arguing incessantly with his morally upright father, and stealing to buy drugs when he could not persuade his mother to support his habit. After each arrest, his mother would plead with the authorities to give him another chance, protesting that he was basically a good boy with evil companions. Nevertheless, she was relieved when he was in jail, because he was out of circulation and out of trouble.

The *first symptoms* of her illness began shortly after he was released from prison. She knew that soon the household would again be disrupted and that he would resume drug dealing. A close woman friend died suddenly. This left her without an established significant other, since neither her husband nor her daughter offered much support, only gratuitous and punitive advice about her son. Incidentally, those who are interested in anniversary reactions will want to know that her son was sent to prison for parole violation, her daughter left her husband and returned home, and the patient's brother died of cancer—all in the month of April, not in the same year, of course.

FGG

I saw the patient about twenty times before her transfer. She was a good talker, and spontaneously said that her symptoms started the same day she bailed her son out of jail. But this is a slightly different version from the one JPL just mentioned. True, she knew he'd get in trouble. But she was always ready to bail him out, in more ways than one. "What's a mother to do?" she would ask, over and over. Much as she loathed the turmoil at home and was sure that he'd begin dealing in drugs, it was better to have him out of jail. At least that's how she expressed it to me.

I can't summarize all of our contacts, but it was sometimes hard to know if she were speaking about her son or her illness. Maybe they were the same. For example, she didn't want to go home, because she dreaded the fights between her husband and son. But she didn't want to go to the chronic care hospital, either, because it signified failure of treatment and inevitable death. She had similar ideas about her son. She didn't want him at home, but also resisted the inescapable notion that he was incorrigible—incurable, if you will—and wanted him out of prison as long as possible. She persisted with a kind of parallel denial, hoping for his reformation and her recovery. When it became apparent that neither would happen, she tended to blame everything on his drugs and her medications. She had received several courses of chemotherapy. So you can see how closely identified this woman was with her errant son.

Perhaps our visitors can add something at this point.

IP-1

The patient knew her diagnosis, why she received chemotherapy, and the significance of her chronic care hospitalization. She asked me several times, "How much time do I have?" I thought she meant how much longer she'd live, although this is a rather infrequent question among people who are fatally ill.

You see, I took care of her during the periods between general hospital admissions, and made arrangements for her follow-up clinic visits, as well as a few other things. Her question really meant two other things beside death: How long could she stay outside of a chronic care hospital? This is a little different from asking how long she had to live. The other meaning of how much time referred to her son. When would his probation be revoked again? In a word, I thought, her freedom from the confines of a chronic care hospital matched her concern about her son's freedom. In both cases, freedom from confinement was temporary and provisional.

Finally, home problems became so difficult that she even asked to go to the chronic care hospital. Meanwhile, because beds weren't available, she had to wait. We brought in a practical nurse and a homemaker. The patient herself just gave up during the waiting period. In contrast with her usual self, sociable, talkative, self-reliant, she seemed unwilling or unable to do almost anything. I can't emphasize this drastic change sufficiently. From absolute openness and concern for others, she lapsed into withdrawal and invalidism. After several weeks in limbo, arrangements were completed and transfer was imminent. She brightened up immediately. It was as if now a phase of her life was left behind. Miss ——— was her social worker in the chronic hospital.

IP-2

Yes, I followed her for about four months until she died. Let me first describe our setup in the hospital, because the surroundings were very important to this lady.

When first admitted, our bed shortage made it necessary to put her in a two-bed room, located in what is largely a male section of the hospital. The head nurse of that section is very bright and sympathetic. She cares about her patients deeply. She talks with families openly about various problems. Her attitude inspires other nurses to that service. They are equally supportive to terminal patients.

I noticed that she identified her illness with her son's antisocial behavior. She wasn't depressed, and spoke about her son as simply a "bad boy," not an incorrigible drug pusher. Both her cure and her son's rehabilitation would take a long time, but were bound to happen.

An unfortunate series of events ended this early period of well-being. About midway in her hospitalization, one of the resident doctors, not her own, was on call, and stopped to chat with her. Because she felt well, and gave him such a favorable report, he commented casually that she might start thinking about going home soon. She promptly became depressed. She also denied flatly that she had ever been told about her illness, whether it was the diagnosis, treatment, or outlook. However, with additional support, the denial and depression were simultaneously relieved within a day or two. She then asked for a lawyer, because she had set aside a fund for her funeral in a savings account, and was afraid that her son might get hold of it and spend the money on drugs. Once again, I suppose, there is a paradox between denying her illness and at the same time, or shortly after, asking for a lawyer to prepare for her funeral.

FGG

This paradox is called *middle knowledge*. A terminal patient may suddenly deny any illness whatsoever, and even start making unrealistic plans for the future. I am told that in the old days, patients with advanced tuberculosis would show something like middle knowledge, shortly before death.

RSS

Is middle knowledge like premortem clarity?

FGG

Not exactly. Middle knowledge is uncertain certainty, an intermediate zone between awareness and denial. Premortem clarity is just that. No denial is necessary.

IP-2

Well, to continue my story. Her depression cleared, and she seemed to accept the entire situation. Then, something good happened! You see, we have a training program for chaplains at our hospital. A young seminarian called on her, and they hit it off right away. In fact, she was invited to appear before the entire group, where she was interviewed and spoke up very articulately. At the conclusion, in response to her acceptance of the situation, the assemblage stood up and applauded.

The essence of the message they gave her was that while her family had done some bad things, she was a very good mother. Under trying, difficult circumstances, she had managed to help others and accomplish a great deal, regardless of her son. I don't think we could have ordered a more appreciative response or a more spontaneous testimonial. Her sense of worth zoomed.

I wish that all had gone well after that. It didn't. For some reason, call it "administrative convenience," she was moved from the supportive two-bed situation on the "good" ward to a less desirable section of the hospital. The head nurse is of the so-called old school, who believes in taking physical care of patients, but brusquely, and with a no-nonsense attitude, quite different from the personal support she got at first. Incidentally, her son was again apprehended and sent to jail about this time. There might be some connection. But actually, very little time was left. Her depression upon being moved against her will deepened into withdrawal, just as it had at home, while waiting for a bed. She also became confused, and complained that everyone she saw was a stranger, which, of course, they were. Yes, the transfer to the bad ward was in mid-April!

During lucid moments, her attitude was one of fatalistic surrender. She would do whatever God willed, but she said it with what I surmise was the way she told Dr. FGG, "What's a mother to do?" Her family wasn't much help. They complained a great deal about nothing very specific. After her death, autopsy was refused.

* * *

ADW

Now, if everyone is clear, and there aren't any further questions, we can hear about the psychological tests.

LCJ

I tested the patient at home, during that discouraging period between discharge from this hospital and admission to the next. I must have caught her on a good day, because it was fairly easy to engage her in conversation. She dated all her symptoms from a clinic visit about six months before. There was a doctor who seemed very businesslike. He didn't listen, asked her a few brusque physical questions, and came across as indifferent to everything except her symptoms. Obviously, she had to have symptoms to go to the clinic in the first place. But it does show how sensitive this woman was to implied rebuffs from authority. She liked to talk and enjoyed being appreciated. She cooperated fully in the tests [results were given]. The main theme was an abiding faith in self-sufficiency and in being helped by helping others. Nevertheless, there was an equally clear idea expressed that all her hopes and faith had been in vain.

MLV

Just like in the hospital . . . she was so sure about getting well that the nurses wondered if she knew or understood anything about her illness. But the doctors had gone over the facts several times.

HSO

When any patient denies so strongly, it is very hard for a doctor or nurse to contradict them. We may even go along with the denial; we know better, but it may be just too painful to disenchant what seems to be working well. A patient is very hopeful, and it makes us ashamed to prick the bubble of illusion. I admit these feelings from time to time, but we should be careful that we lead the patient back to the way things actually are. Otherwise, we conspire to fool the patient, and this leads to estrangement.

Now, while I have the floor, I want to jump ahead to the terminal events. I agree that she began to die when she was transferred to that strange and uncongenial ward. No one really spoke with her, and naturally she was confused and depressed. Whenever a patient says that everyone and everything seem strange, I interpret it as a form of depersonalization. More commonly, they just cannot make their needs known and believe that no one cares, that everyone is indifferent. So in their confusion, the world disappears as it has been known. Estrangement and alienation creep in.

LCJ

Real or not, she dated her initial symptoms from her contact—or lack of contact—with the unsympathetic clinic doctor. Much later, she went downhill while on the bad or indifferent ward which was presided over by the brusque, old-school nurse. I think this is consistent with the other story that her symptoms began when her son was released from prison. He was on the streets and at home again, but trouble was certain. Nothing could be done about it, and we have already heard how fatalistic and frustrated she became near the end. Actually, she showed more anxiety and anger during tests than she showed depression. Recall that this woman always tried to please other people, and responded so much to signs of appreciation. I regard this as a reaction formation against resentment, and her tests show plenty of anger. Listen to this. She says, "You pray, do the best you can, help everyone, but nothing happens, nothing works out. I'll do whatever God wants, but it might not do any good." I call this strategy, submission to the inevitable. When she was transferred from the good ward to the bad ward, she could no longer struggle. At best, she submitted, but actually, I think, it was resignation and depression, not acceptance.

ADW

Most of us are familiar with the syndrome, Giving up/Given up, described by Engel and Schmale. Note how closely fluctuations of her illness corresponded to her son's releases and confinements, in jail or on the street. When did she give up on him?

IP-2

I remember that shortly before her transfer to the bad ward, or maybe it was just afterward, she got a letter from her son. As a rule, his letters were to plead for money; he never visited her, to my knowledge. This time, however, she refused to open the letter, and asked that it be returned to him. I call this giving up in the sense you mean.

ADW

And she would also give up on herself at the same time. As HSO said, this was estrangement at worst, fatalism, at best. I call it being alienated and angry, confused and anxious.

JWW

What were the real precipitants in this case?

ADW

You said precipitants, not simply precursors. Precipitants are not causes, because I don't think we can use the concept of "cause" in dealing with psychosocial events. Rather, we should talk about clusters of events, psychological, social, and physical. It is well-known that certain people become physically ill around the time of stressful events. It is not an invariable relationship. I suspect that it is true for some people, but perhaps not so common in others. People with much depression, those with a lot of anxiety, are apt to recall and report different events. There is also a difference between observation made on-the-spot, and retrospective reports of patients. And, of course, the big danger is reductionism. I am a firm believer in nonexcludability! Precipitants in this case were undoubtedly her son's repeated incarcerations and releases, until she finally gave up on him, and not incidentally, on herself. But she also responded adversely to situations in which someone was indifferent, impatient, or very callous. Note the clinic doctor and the hard-boiled hospital nurse. Good works and good intentions just don't pay off. Her formula fails, and vulnerability increases.

HSO

What could we have done to improve the situation, since we couldn't have controlled the hospital administration nor reformed her son? It all sounds very deterministic.

JWW

Fate probably does sit in, but remember that the concept of clustering applies only to some patients, not to all. With this woman, estrangement wasn't necessary—recall how well she responded to the approval of the seminarians. Even our accessibility changes the psychosocial network a little.

FGG

I might have seen her more often, but we don't know how the relation with the young chaplain went, after the conference. Estrangement, disengagement, and clustering are, after all, simply the names we give to a series of distressing events, maybe to how badly we treat some patients.

ADW

Reality testing can't work well, when reality lets a patient down. A patient who is vulnerable will be damaged by episodes that might be coped with readily at other times. Safe conduct during the terminal period is crucial, but we rarely plan ahead with a particular patient in mind. With this patient, she needed someone to hear her out, and then to "applaud" in a silent appreciation. Very little more.

Case 2. Dying and Denial

ADW

The patient today was a sixty-one-year-old factory mechanic who was admitted to the hospital six weeks before death. He claimed to have had no symptoms until two months preceding admission. Despite rapid and severe weight loss, gross abdominal distention, indicative of ascites and liver metastases, and signs of intestinal obstruction, he denied almost every symptom until the very end. Physical deterioration was so advanced that it underscored his mental state, which was one of most remarkable denial.

JPL

He was the last male of a large family. Two of his brothers had died of malignancies within five years. The patient's wife told me that he was afraid of getting cancer for many years, but after admission to the hospital, it was never mentioned again. The entire family was said to be quietly self-sufficient and hard-working, without many outside interests. They were all afraid of doctors, and this may account for the long lapse before he was finally induced to come into the hospital.

The couple had no children. Their hobby was raising dogs. One of their favorite dogs died two years before, around the time that a brother died of cancer. The patient brooded for a long time after these deaths, and was even less interested in outside events. He responded slightly when spoken to at home, and we can presume that he was suffering from a fairly severe depression. Then the company he worked for went on strike, and never reopened. He had been at this company since he first went to work at age fifteen.

And, to illustrate the theory of clusters, or that troubles often run together, a close friend (he didn't have many) and a brother-in-law both died of cancer in the past year.

I would say that all this constituted a substantial number of precursors.

IP

I was the social worker who followed this man during hospitalization.

Despite his enormous, swollen abdomen and obvious illness, with tubes running out and into him, he did not indicate—at any time—that he was even moderately worried, anxious, or depressed. He told me about his job, but did not report that the company had closed permanently or temporarily. In fact, he gave the impression that his job was more important than it actually had been. He looked forward to getting better (from a slight indisposition) and returning to work in this nonexistent company.

His optimism and composure were so deceptive or convincing that despite the appearance of advanced illness, I didn't realize myself how sick he was, or how terminal his illness was. In fact, on the day before he died $(D-1)$, I was pleased to tell the patient and his wife that the insurance company had agreed to pay for his care after hospital discharge. The patient himself had talked about going to a rehabilitation hospital (yes, a contradiction from the "slight indisposition") and even about retirement (a contradiction from his earlier plan for returning to work).

Now I do recall something else. On the day he died, his wife and two sisters were sitting quietly at the bedside. I went into the room, and because no one was saying a word, I assumed he was asleep. I said that I'd come back in fifteen minutes. Maybe I took a little longer, but no more than twenty. Anyway, when I returned, the women had already gone; the patient had died, and they had told the head nurse very simply that they now had to make funeral arrangements.

This seems very strange. Not just because they hadn't made arrangements beforehand. Most families linger a little after a death, talk to the nurses, thank them, and even show some outward feelings. Not here. They just went away. I had talked with the wife and patient a good deal, but she didn't wait to see me again, either. Was this appropriate behavior for people who had been denying a serious illness?

HSO

I call this behavior consistent, but not appropriate. My contact with the patient began two weeks after admission, a month before death. He was always very cordial, but told me only the most impersonal facts about himself, other than those he covered with denial. For example, he claimed to have been entirely well until two months before entering the hospital. Then a slight back pain started. A friend "just up and died." This was the close friend we later learned had died of cancer, as had two of his brothers. The dates were also incorrectly given, if the times of these deaths were accurately given by his wife. I asked about his two brothers. The patient said that their illnesses had been contracted at work. One brother had been struck in the chest, then developed lung cancer. The other brother worked in a printing plant. Exposure to dyes, paints, and ink led to leukemia. Then he quickly added that he, too, had been around paint and dyes, and had sustained blows to his chest, but through the years was free of any illness. In a single verbal stroke, he disclosed that two brothers died of cancer, but separated himself by saying that he had undergone the same risks and had not contracted fatal illness. Therefore, he was well.

The closest he came to acknowledging how sick he was came during a period when doctors debated about whether or not to operate for his intestinal obstruction. They set the time for an exploratory, then put it off. In response to their delay or indecision, maybe both, the patient said that if they postponed operating again, he would face surgery on the day before Memorial Day, and this might not be a good sign. He was so jocular, as a rule, that this was construed as humor, not worry. Anyway, he was operated on. Four days later, he was very sick, rapidly declining, but still very optimistic. When the stitches come out, he said, he'd be able to eat, put on weight, get better, and go home. At this time, he looked like the textbook picture of terminal cachexia. He did not complain of pain, but got morphine every eight hours, anyway.

MLV

I confirm that. The nurses were almost angry at him because his joking manner was so inappropriate with his physical condition. One time, for example, he had a rather arduous trip down to the radiology department for a barium swallow. He was partially obstructed even after the operation. But he reported laughingly about the barium swallow that he'd just had a chocolate soda. On the day before death, he would only report that he was "not too well," but added that a good cathartic would fix him up.

JPL

My informants told me that on the outside he was a rather dour man, not given to conversation, and seldom laughed or joked, not as he did in the hospital. It is quite true that he didn't complain about pain, either at home or in the hospital. There was a bit of backache, nothing more.

ADW

Here is a case of major denial—of almost everything, not just of illness, but of other events in his life, his work, the reasons given for his brothers' deaths. Add to this the tendency to laugh it off during the terminal stage.

With all our talk about terminal patients who are eager to "discuss their demise," this man is certainly an outstanding exception. Dr. HSO offered him many opportunities to talk, even probing a bit. His denial was like a wall. And he had no prominent symptoms, despite severe terminal signs.

*   *   *

LCJ

Now, in view of this patient's global, uncompromising denial, which you clinicians seem to find so startling, I'm sure that the psychological test results will be equally interesting. It was filled with voluminous references to death, dying, depression, suicide, suffering, and even included some historical information. It showed everything we looked for clinically, and had been unable to find.

Let me just cite a couple of examples which contrast with his denial, optimism, and joking air. "Short suffering is better than long illness. Lots of times, when a man gets very depressed, if he had someone to talk to, a counselor, maybe he wouldn't have to kill himself!" After this comment, he paused, looked out of the window, and then told me about a fellow worker who had gotten in debt, and killed himself by jumping eight years before. He talked about his two brothers and about cancer. He also said that two weeks before his hospital admission, the son of the man who suicided eight years ago also died of cancer!

None of this came through in the interviews. But now I must also report that in his POMS, he lapsed into denial, admitting only to happiness. No anger, tension, or depression.

JPL

On one occasion he whispered to his wife that all the fellows in his four-bed room had cancer. But then he quickly corrected himself, saying, "If I had cancer, I'd want to die right away." From time to time he said things like, "If the doctors aren't sure about operating, maybe they aren't sure what's wrong with me." But another time he said, gloomily, if they don't hurry up and decide what to do, they shouldn't bother. He never, to my knowledge, mentioned suicide.

His wife always talked about him in the past tense, as if he were already dead. Maybe that's why she and his sisters left so promptly after he died.

ADW

We are accustomed to finding that the staff supports a patient's denial. It is surprising to learn that the nurses were disturbed, even angry, about his hard-core denial. Glaser and Strauss found that the staff might be impatient or angry if a dying patient lives beyond an expected schedule or trajectory. I see no theoretical reason why it would not also apply to a terminal patient who refused to be terminal in his attitude. Where did the reinforcement for denial come from?

Denial or the act of dying, which is somewhat more processlike, is generally a social strategy, designed to preserve a relationship. This might have been true for our patient at home, but according to MLV's report and HSO's observations, it was not true in the hospital. However, what if this man could talk freely about his brothers, friends, hospital roommates, who had cancer? Wouldn't this alienate people? Not here because nurses and HSO would have been very willing to hear him out. We can presume that he was depressed for at least a year or more, since the closing of his factory, death of friends and brother, and also the death of the favorite dog. He had few, if any symptoms, and permitted his illness to race ahead before reluctantly seeking any medical attention. Then, once in the hospital, he joked and laughed with nurses, and when speaking to HSO, the death doctor, kept things on a very impersonal plane. He even denied the problem of permanent unemployment, and the kind of job he had held.

RSS

Did denial help this man? Many people would argue that his few symptoms and unwavering confidence in recovery were good things, and that talking openly about death could only make him worse, especially since he was going to die anyway. Why not just take him on his own terms?

FGG

Usually it is our hang-ups that prevent us from confronting a patient with his poor outlook. That wasn't the case here. This patient was a denier, but he also repressed, if we assume that the psychological tests brought out death themes, like suicide, suffering, and so forth.

JWW

That is another issue. On one hand, his denial seemed to prevent undue suffering. His preoccupation with death themes certainly did not lead to any suicide attempts. For him, adamant denial worked. But could we have imposed or strengthened denial, if we were so inclined?

ADW

This is an essential point in psychological management. We are often cautioned about probing patients too deeply, lest we precipitate a serious depression. This man had already been depressed, but showed no signs of it after admission to the hospital. Either his remission took place when he came here, that is, he became less depressed, or the physical illness itself somehow relieved his depression. Somehow I can't argue either side very vigorously. Should we have pushed this patient harder for his death themes? To what end? He had not been lied to, so there is no problem of alienation as a result of falsehoods. He was not a man who depended upon a great many significant others. His wife and sisters were still with him. I suspect that the matter was settled within the family, and that others were excluded.

JPL

When I spoke with his widow recently she told me that he had given instructions about what he wanted to wear at his funeral. I suppose we could interpret this to mean that he didn't believe in his own death, but in everything up to his death. Dr. ADW calls this third-stage denial. But it is now more obvious that his denial was most in evidence in the context of the hospital. He shut people out by impersonalizing, and shut them off by joking with nurses.

ADW

What have we learned about denial that we didn't know before?

Perhaps it is surprising that projective tests can reveal death themes that clinical interviews cannot. Feifel and his colleagues have shown that when a topic like death is repressed, and even when fear of death is denied, death anxiety returns anyway and can be caught by testing.

I suppose it is practical to recognize that some patients do deny more than they accept the realities of fatal illness. In fact, denial and acceptance seem to be interwoven more often than they are separated. Our methods of diagnosis impose a kind of categorical all-or-none upon denial and acceptance; patients may not. If his denial had interfered with proper treatment—suppose he had wanted to sign out, or something that definitely would have been harmful —then more pushing would be indicated.

FGG

Suppose we had asked him, "How sick are you?" What would he have answered?

HSO

I did, and I told you. I think that this man had already come to terms with death. He had spoken about the funeral. The family was very controlled and self-sufficient. Grief was at a low level. This man didn't trust the medical profession. Why he unburdened himself to the psychologist, I don't know. All I know was that his talk with me was very thin and impersonal. I was never close to death themes in my interviews.

IP

I had the same feelings in my entire contact with the family.

RSS

Given another patient just like this man, would you push harder, insist upon more candor, and so forth?

ADW

In all candor, no.

Case 3. Psychosocial Stages in Death and Dying

ADW

Thanatology is an "in" topic these days. I won't go into why this might be true, but as you can all testify, we just can't keep up with everything that's being written (please don't try) and all the conferences that are being held. I think that regardless of the bandwagon effect, people should be able to face mortality, especially their own. After all, there are only two deaths that matter to any of us: mine and yours. Other deaths—the impersonal, statistical deaths—are hardly deaths at all. Behind every obituary notice, however, there is a person who became sick and died, a family in bereavement, or a set of circumstances that might have been different. But that's what the psychological autopsy is about. Staging is certainly a prominent concept, too. In trying to describe events carefully, we tend to forget that "stages" are seldom as precisely defined as we would like. Patients rarely conform to the staging procedure in every respect. We lapse into the magic of naming. To give something a name is an ancient device for getting control over it. Stages are not equivalent to the process of dying, or, before you remind me of my mistake, living until death.

What processes are "normal" for people who are dying? The chief advantage of describing stages, I think, is to set the stage for a better death. Obviously, people change and prepare themselves in different ways. These changes take place within time intervals, but chronological time is not the same as psychosocial time.

The difference between them is the difference between a calendar and a schedule. Case 2 showed us that denial can be militantly maintained throughout an illness to the very end. Some of our other cases, however, started with acceptance, and ended with denial, but most seemed to show mixtures of acceptance and denial from time to time, from person to person. It's hard to monitor stages in patients who eventually die, unless we start observation at a fairly advanced chronological time. More of that later. Let's turn to today's case. In a word, he survived a craniotomy for a brain tumor, and went through a discouraging period of rehabilitation for fifteen years. Then he developed cancer of the colon with extensive metastases, and died within three months. I thought that because of the long interval between separate malignancies this patient might tell us something about staging and preparation.

JPL

We have a lot of information about this patient. He had been admitted to the MGH on eight occasions. I am not sure we'll be able to answer the questions that Dr. ADW raised.

He was aged fifty-four at the time of death, married twenty-five years, father of five sons, stepfather of one daughter. Although he and his wife never separated, they argued a great deal. I suppose you could call it an "emotional divorce," because they seemed to live mutually isolated lives under the same roof.

He drank to excess at times, as his father did before. But when he married, he gave up alcohol, and even during what must have been a very trying period of convalescence and rehabilitation, remained an abstainer.

He had two close men friends. One died shortly before he developed the brain tumor, and the other died of cancer three years later. He was a loner both at work and throughout most of his life. Of course, he couldn't work for a long time, but even so, he wasn't close with any of his sons, several of whom drank excessively and had brushes with the law.

My interviews were with his wife and stepdaughter. In fact, the stepdaughter was a better observer, knew him better as a person, and got along with him better than anyone else. She described him as a hard worker who never got much of anything from his life—neither satisfaction nor material gains. This trait carried over to his rehabilitation programs, which he worked hard at, without much payoff.

His wife had little to say, except that she didn't want him to know about the bowel cancer "because he might lose hope and kill himself." This seemed a little strange; he evidently hadn't lost hope during the preceding fifteen years, and had never attempted suicide.

The stepdaughter indicated that the patient had changed recently. One day he accidentally flushed his dentures down the toilet. He refused to replace the teeth, and became more depressed, stating that he was just too tired to chew his food. Lack of dentures and excessive fatigue were given as the explanation of severe weight loss, a good example of first-order denial with rationalization.

HSO

My sessions were brief and unproductive. I saw him six days before death $(D-6)$. He was grossly emaciated, with a protuberant abdomen. Whether or not his wife thought so, he knew the diagnosis, but fluctuated in the

degree of accessibility. Sometimes, I learned, his knowledge of having terminal cancer came out in unusual
ways. For example, one night he was playing a word
game with several nurses. When he picked up the letter
A, he said, "I have arthritis." He then touched the letter
B, saying, "I once had a brain tumor." After a brief
pause, he pointed to the letter *C*, and stated, "If I have
cancer, I want to know about it." This "middle knowledge," as I see it, meant that he was certain about
arthritis, knew he once had a brain tumor, but stipu-
lated "If I have cancer ..." I remind you that this
episode occurred when time was very short.

Our contacts were curious, in a way. He insisted
upon reminiscing about his former work, which he had
not done for many years, but then indirectly clarified
why he was thinking about work. He said, "It isn't as if I
came in contact with poisons ..."

When I returned, he was a little suspicious, not as
cordial. I explained. Then he became very literal, saying
that the body is like an automobile. If something's
wrong, you take it to the garage, let the mechanics work
on it, until the car is running again. The same with him.
He eats, sleeps, takes medicine, and does not work. He
had another strategy for avoiding the imminence of
death. The MGH is an outstanding hospital. If he
couldn't be cured, they would send him somewhere else.
Ergo, since he's still here, he must be getting better.
This was the $D-5$ day. Afterward, when I persisted, he
simply brushed me off.

JWW

Four days before death $(D-4)$, I gave him psychological tests.

He was cooperative up to a point, but stalled from time to time. He was not heavily sedated. Two themes permeated the TAT stories: (1) Does perseverance pay off, or does it end in "garbage"? (2) People want to leave, but are held back. Or, in contrast, someone doesn't want to leave, and needs encouragement to go on. In one story, he talked about an overbearing mother, and implied that if he'd married someone else, maybe more like his stepdaughter, life might have been different. But he didn't complain.

FGG

This man had every reason to complain, but he didn't. He was essentially symptom-free, except for weight loss. Dr. Kubler-Ross has described certain stages of dying that some people think are prototypes: denial, anger, bargaining, depression, and acceptance. As I understand them, they tend to occur in that order. What I see in this man is denial, very little else. In other words, at the end of a long, long struggle, he seems to be denying more than ever! I notice that on the day before his death he went for a ride with his wife and stepdaughter. He returned without complaints, and actually said he had a very good weekend—no depression, no symptoms, no questions, and evidently no premonitions or explicit acceptance.

JWW

His denial wasn't limited to the illness. When Dr. HSO probed, the patient became a little annoyed, a touch of anger, perhaps, but nothing about the illness, only his work of long ago.

Here is another terminal patient who is reluctant to

admit very much about his situation. How many exceptions are there?

HSO

Remember that he was a loner. And he was more
open with some people at different times, if not with
me. I must confess that because he looked like a
cadaver, I asked questions, hoping he wouldn't answer.
Maybe I reinforced his control.

I don't know when Kubler-Ross stages begin. I
presume they start when the patient is first interviewed.
Other patients we have talked about begin with acceptance, and end with denial, or fail to show any bargaining or anger whatsoever.

ADW

Remember that the reason we are discussing this
man is because he had already been through a serious
illness. Fifteen years of rehabilitation programs after a
brain tumor should not have left him with many illu-
sions. As I understand it, he cooperated in efforts to
train him for other work, but nothing turned out well.
He apparently preferred to think of himself as an
automobile that needed repairs. But he didn't think that
he was beyond repair.

HSO

Despite the glowing reports of his last weekend,
things were not good at home. On the seventh admission, one month before death $(D-30)$, he was sad and
discouraged, according to the record. He wanted to go
home. This request was granted, but within 24 hours he
was back here for the eighth admission, the last, be-

cause his wife found him too difficult to care for. I suspect that this might have contributed to the denial and unnatural optimism that I found, just six days before death. So perhaps underneath the denial, there was exhaustion and acceptance.

ADW

Well, what "stage" was he in? Look how difficult it is to isolate a single characteristic, denial, depression, anger, and so forth, and make pronouncements about process.

IP

I'd like to tell the group about a patient I followed for several years. I'll be very brief, but the case illustrates what Dr. ADW called the principle of nonexcludability.

She was a fifty-eight-year-old schoolteacher, who lived with another unmarried sister until about one year before her sister died of carcinoma of the breast. My patient always had regular physical checkups, but she insisted upon getting another opinion after her family doctor seemed to dismiss the significance of a breast lump. There was no denial here.

The biopsy by a second physician showed an intraductal carcinoma with many positive axillary lymph nodes. She had a radical mastectomy. I saw her first about two weeks later. She was feeling very well, but was cautious about her future. She returned to schoolteaching, despite fatigue, but nothing I would call depression. Several months later she received radiation therapy, which did make her depressed. She was more fatigued than ever.

Two months after the radiation therapy ended, she developed a cough which doctors treated symptomatically. Finally, in exasperation, she went to another clinic, had a chest x-ray, and was found to have pneumonitis. She then became very angry at the doctors who operated on her and at the radiation therapist. Quite rightly, I think, she expected them to show more interest in her, to talk about possible complications, to take her seriously, because she had gone along with everything they had recommended. This was anger, but it was not based on the presence of the tumor, but on the seeming indifference of the doctors. I would not call this the "stage of anger." Then she was transferred to a new school. Everything was different; people were strangers, and she wondered why the superintendent had shifted her at this time. She was lonely, friendless, and, I suppose, depressed again.

Her pneumonitis did not clear up entirely. She continued to cough, but did not insist upon further x-rays. I saw her from time to time over the following months. She wanted to finish the school year in order to be eligible for a pension. There was acceptance of her physical condition but there was no apparent spread of the primary tumor. Anyway, the academic year ended. She retired, and the last time I heard from her was a friendly holiday card, which did not mention the illness.

FGG

What about the terminal period?

IP

There wasn't any. I just wanted to point out that the idea of staging psychosocial episodes is very artificial.

Had I not known about the exogenous events, such as the doctor who evidently did a little denying himself, and the inner resentment because of the radiation therapist's failure to talk with her, I might have focused on her emotional state, and not fully realized that she was simply coping with problems that were secondarily related to the threat of death. Actually, at no time did she deny the possibility of relapse or that she might not recover.

ADW

Thank you for mentioning this case. It shows that patients cope and fail to cope with various problems, and that their emotional responses are simply indicators of personal conflict and crises. Because these responses occur in a cancer patient, or one with myocardial infarction, or whatever, does not mean that denial, depression, anger, etc., stem from the imminence or awareness of mortality.

We usually find what we're looking for. For example, I believe that patients with fatal illnesses will talk about themselves, at least more than some people looking after them care to admit. But look how I cling to that idea—we have had several exceptions to this principle, and I salvage the general idea by successive qualifications.

When I find a dying patient who does not respond to an interview approach, and refuses to acknowledge my open-ear policy, I suspect that the patient is denying the fact of fatal illness and does not want to talk with me, but might talk with someone else. It is seldom that any patient talks and talks about death. We should recognize that, in the preterminal and terminal stages of fatal illness, many patients have problems yielding control to others. So they may fight, criticize, want to go home, despite contraindications. Others may give up, and simply accept whatever comes.

The concept of psychosocial staging appeals to me, because patients are apt to have social and emotional problems anyway. And some of these problems—call them crises, if you wish—may be more prevalent early in an illness than later on. Furthermore, it would be very orderly if psychosocial issues followed as neatly as anatomical and clinical staging seem to do. I believe that patients do cope according to their available strategies, but that there is no well-recognized succession of emotional responses which are typical of people facing incipient death. But, once again, we can usually find illustrative cases, especially if we're trying to support our own hypotheses.

Look, if we were to accept the reality of successive stages that occur in most dying patients, the same order might also apply to the stages of, say, bereavement —denial, anger, bargaining, depression, acceptance. Or to someone who has just lost his job. We are always dealing with evolving processes, which means that for every problem, there is a predominant coping strategy, which sometimes works, and at other times, fails. Our job as thanatologists is to discriminate between problems, trying to see which ones are specific to the illness, and which are simply secondary complications of the human condition.

Case 4. Precursors and Precipitants of Suicide

ADW

It is said that at one time or another, most people have thoughts of suicide. These are evidently low-lethality thoughts because actual attempts are comparatively infrequent. Suicide is a leading cause of death, especially among the young adult population, because they are less prone to die of other causes.

The actual incidence of suicide, whether completed or attempted, does not convey the enormity of the problem. From a human viewpoint it is a tragedy; from the viewpoint of coping, it is largely a sign of ineffectiveness and failure. I have compared suicide to war and bankruptcy. Both are strategies for coping with extreme conditions, but they are extreme measures in themselves, and not a sign of freedom to act.

The suicidal act is difficult to comprehend. Few people who have attempted suicide and survive can adequately describe their presuicidal state of mind. Even the precursors and precipitants often seem inappropriate and banal for such a drastic form of behavior.

The case today will illustrate the suicidal context, not the specific causation of suicide.

FGG

Here are the clinical facts. The patient was a twenty-seven-year-old officer in the maritime services. During an extended cruise, he slashed his wrists, stabbed himself with a scissors, and threw himself in front of an oncoming truck.

JPL

Here are some psychosocial facts. The patient is the second of three children. But he was born while his father was on active duty overseas during World War II. So there has always been a question of paternity, at least in his father's mind.

Despite years of emotional divorce, his parents shared the same room until very recently. His father would disappear from time to time, and his whereabouts would be unknown. He was away for three years on one such disappearance. But when he returned, it was without explanation. No questions were asked. Several of these episodes took place during the patient's childhood. There were also frequent moves from one town to another. I wanted to check with the patient's father, but he refused to see me. He is said to be very secretive and suspicious. However, he supported the household; he was disinterested in other family matters.

About a year ago, the patient's mother developed a duodenal ulcer. A few months later, she and his father decided to be divorced at last, officially, after many separations and quarrels. Following this decision, they continued to live in the same house, and her health did not improve. At the time that our patient shipped out on an unexpectedly prolonged cruise, she was scheduled to enter a local hospital for a hysterectomy and, possibly, gastrointestinal surgery for the ulcer. So, when he left, there was considerable doubt and uncertainty both about his mother's health and prospective surgery, and the final breakup of the household.

In contrast with his father, who did not even meet his son's plane at the airport when he returned from overseas after the suicide attempt, his mother was very cooperative. She reported many facts about our patient, but in summary, he was dominated by his father, as were the other children, and was very passive and seclusive throughout childhood. He had few close friends, dated rarely, and had only passing interest in hobbies and sports. His school record was mediocre.

The decision to attend merchant marine school was made by his father. The patient had dropped out of regular school, stayed at home, without plans for his future. He was accepted and seems to have fulfilled requirements for graduation, four years ago. However, it is reported that one month before graduating, seven classmates drowned under circumstances that were never clarified. One year ago, around the time that his parents decided to divorce, his closest friend, maybe his only friend, was killed while at sea. It was rumored that he had known too much about certain forms of corruption in various organizations related to the merchant marine. I have no further details about this matter.

Here are some precursors, then. A seclusive boy grows to manhood, dominated by his indifferent father, who picks out a career for his son to follow. There are mysterious drownings, and his best friend is killed. About the trip he was on: it was supposed to be only a short, shakedown cruise, but it stretched into many months. During this time, he had no communication about his parents, their marriage, the family, or his mother's health after surgery.

FGG

The trip, as mentioned, was supposed to last only a few weeks, but it went on for five months. No reasons were given.

To continue: the patient becomes more and more isolated and nervous. He does not know what is happening at home nor where his destination will be. The first mate is a suspicious and domineering man who foments resentment in the crew that reaches almost mutinous proportions. —Yes, yes, just like his father.

His job on board the ship is to be in charge of the boilers. He is a low-grade officer, and by rank and inclination, seems to have been affiliated with neither the crew nor the other officers.

The boilers are old, and break down. But the ship continues on this extended trip. The ship slows, the men become more and more disgruntled and rebellious. There are two versions of the situation on shipboard. In one story, the men refused to work because of the first mate and his bullying attitude. In the second story, the men were not permitted to work overtime and earn more money. Instead, the officers took on the extra work and were paid accordingly.

The patient is caught in-between the officers and crew. More and more decisions are forced on him. He can patch up the boilers and continue the trip, allowing officers to earn more but thereby increasing the crew's resentment. Or he could report that the boilers are too defective to repair. The crew wanted him to do this, and contributed their share by doing a poor job on the repairs he ordered. But if the ship put into port, the officers would be antagonized.

Still more trouble appears. Two months before the suicide attempt, another mate comes aboard. He is suspected of being a union informer, out to get the troublemakers. Recall what happened to his best friend, and why . . . I urge you to think about this, not as a factual account (I am not qualified or informed about that) but as to our patient's reality in the presuicidal period.

Still more troubles . . . During many idle hours, the crew loafs around, openly resenting the extra pay earned by officers. The men pass around some pornography. The patient reads about homosexuality, and becomes so upset that he desists from masturbating for over two months, something of a record for him. And about that time, the suspected informer comes aboard.

All these things are now coming to a boiling point: increasing workload, identity confusion, suspected of not doing his job, not sure what his job should be, in the dark about his family, uncertain about how long the trip will last, not knowing his destination, problems of anxiety and homosexuality. I should insert here that the patient never dated (maybe occasionally), had one homosexual contact at age fourteen, and was as much a sexual enigma to himself as he was to us.

To continue, for several days and nights preceding the attempt, he is forced to stand watch without relief. There is sleep deprivation, he becomes more fatigued, more apprehensive about making a mistake, and thinks anything he might do could be a mistake. He is too agitated to sleep when relief does arrive. He appeals to the first mate, but is brusquely rebuffed and sent back to work. Then the boilers break down again.

On the night before the attempt, he starts to imagine that he is to blame for the defective boilers. He becomes almost paralyzed with indecision and fright, believing that everyone is against him. He then turns in desperation to an older member of the crew. This man has been friendly in the past, and because there is no one else, he asks him if he had ever been so nervous. The older man admits that at one time, he had a nervous breakdown and could not go to sea for about nine months. But here he was again. The man reminisces that as a young man he wanted to be a surgeon, but nothing worked out. Now he is resigned to being an ordinary seaman for the rest of his days. Everything is like that, he says, just a series of dreams and disappointments, plans and failures. . . . Suddenly, in the midst of the conversation, our patient walks away, goes to his room, locks the door, and slashes his wrists repeatedly with a razor blade. When the blood starts to flow, he shouts, "No . . . no . . . no," loudly enough to be heard. A voice inside seems to say, "Don't do it!" But he continues to cut. Then there is another voice—we don't know if it came from inside or out—"Get ready, the doctor is coming." He senses that rescue is on its way. So he seizes a scissors and stabs himself in the chest through his clothing. Penetration is slight. Here it is, then: anxiety, indecision, inability to get help, unendurable pressure, fear of being harmed, overwhelmed by a sense of weakness, dreading a permanent state of failure, locking the door but, at the same time, crying out for help.

ADW

It seems to me that Dr. FGG is citing the factors related to a suicide decision, or is it indecision? In one instance, a person may be so demoralized and discouraged that he simply gives up struggling, and decides to end his life. There is little or no equivocation, no effort to reach out or to arrange for a rescue. Such people are often relieved to have made a decision.

There are other instances, however, in which a suicidal act relieves indecision after a long prodromal period of equivocation, anxiety, guilt, or whatever. This patient looked for someone to give direction, and he feared for his life, unable to decide for and by himself. He had few, if any, options. He was cut off, alienated even more than usual from his customary supports, which were in the process of dissolving, anyway. I guess he shows signs of more indecision than of a frank decision to end his life. The older seaman precipitated the attempt by confirming his empty future. I can't picture this man writing a note in which he would indicate his resolve to die. Instead, he simply tried to cut through the double binds that held him so tenaciously.

FGG

There is more to the story. After the attempt, he was taken to a hospital off the coast of Africa. So his attempt at least forced an end to the tremendous uncertainty, although it would be difficult to call his attempt "manipulative." He was not relieved by hospitalization. In fact, when a doctor approached him in a friendly way, the patient panicked, leaped from his bed, and dashed out into the street. Somehow he had an amorphous notion that he could get back to the states in this way. There was a truck coming down the street, and the patient ran directly into the side of the vehicle. More accurately, he expected or even sought to be hit, but the driver swerved in time to avoid running over the patient. He suffered two broken ribs. Within a few days, plans were made to send him back to the states, with an attendant. Curiously enough, during the flight he asked the attendant directly about homosexuality. The man responded frankly that, yes, he was homosexual. But this candid admission did not accentuate his anxiety; it seemed to clear the air. He settled down and for the rest of the trip was more composed.

IP

I was his therapist on the psychiatric service. He was on the ward only briefly, but showed many of the traits we expected from the description. He was afraid to participate in the ward groups, fearing that he'd lose hold of himself if he responded to the plights and problems of others. To say that he was in quest of a personal or sexual identity would be an understatement. Psychological testing showed persistent themes of fragile, passive women dominated by unfeeling, aggressive men. But the men were also punished for their brutality. Homosexual ideas were secondary, but the idea seemed to be that a homosexual man would not be so aggressive, and it would be safe to be a passive female.

His ward behavior was transparently defensive. He was shy, denied a great deal, and was outwardly aggressive. I suppose he was modeling himself upon the image of unfeeling, tough men. He denied that his parents had any troubles, but later almost pleaded with me to get his parents into family therapy. Above all, he wanted peace and reconciliation at any price. He was unable to foresee any outcome that would be desirable. I thought him to be very vulnerable, paper-thin, subject to recurrent waves of feeling hopeless and worthless. In short, he was a moderately high suicide risk, in my opinion.

JPL

I have checked on his behavior after discharge. The parents continue to stay in the same house, without reconciliation but without formal divorce. His father is out of the house at the moment, and his mother is terrified. The patient just sits around, speaking very little, convinced that he has disgraced the family. He can't leave, doesn't want to, and won't go back to sea.

HSO

Let me suggest an exercise in imagination. Suppose we had been with him in the cabin just before he made the suicide attempt. Knowing what we do now, and assuming that we could turn into anyone we chose, what might have prevented the attempt? I am asking you to imagine yourself as an all-purpose rescuer—what did this man need?

[Participants entered into the spirit of the suggestion, which was dubbed the Proteus Experiment, after the god who could take on any form he wished. Recommendations for the rescuer ranged from becoming a more benevolent first mate who praised him for bearing up under a tremendous burden so heroically, to materializing his father, who told him that even strong men get tired at times, and that he need not be alarmed about homosexual feelings. Mother might take care of him. The ship's company might become reconciled as their destination was made known. Or the captain might decide, once and for all, to turn back to the states. The consensus was that the patient needed rest and absolution from his burden of decision. His suspicion needed to be relieved, and he was to be reassured about the goodwill of the men.]

ADW

A good experiment—it would take a god to undo the mischief. But we frequently err by imagining that suicidal behavior has rational motives, i.e., purposes that can be recognized and, presumably, relieved, were we subtle or powerful enough to do so. Another hypothesis is that suicidal lethality simply reaches a pitch, brought on by physiological and psychosocial deprivations and disorders. For this patient, there was the devil on the bridge in the person of the first mate, and the deep blue sea of nervous breakdown, homosexuality, wasted life, and disgrace. Which part of himself did he want to kill off—the divisiveness aboard, his feeble identity, his sexual problems? Obviously, simple solutions such as being relieved of duty, getting information about home or the next port of call, would not be sufficient. He is still lethal, just sitting around the house, or on the psychiatric ward.

RSS

Can we predict another attempt in the near future, if his lethality remains high and problems are not resolved?

ADW

It doesn't pay to predict the future. Sure, his lethality is moderately high, and certainly nothing has been changed. Even if he seemed to be better able to cope, there would be no guarantee that he wouldn't make another attempt. Prediction of future suicide is very precarious. Studies of people who have attempted suicide come up with the same old precipitants and conflicts—retroflexed hostility, homosexual panic, social alienation, loss of identity, failure to achieve and to hold significant others, and so forth. These are characteristics of people in turmoil and conflict, and are not specific for people on the threshold of attempting suicide. It is true, however, that having attempted suicide before is a fairly reliable indication that a person may do so again, given high enough lethality and low enough controls. I omit the rare case of an altruistic suicide, the ultimate act of freedom. Recent work with biogenic amines and depression suggests that there are specific brain areas serving pleasure and punishment, and we already know about other biochemical studies of suicidal patients. We can only guess. Meanwhile we have to regard suicide risk as a clinical hypothesis, based upon our understanding of individual patients, not upon demographic characteristics.

JWW

Suicide is a fairly uncommon event, but it seems to take place in the setting of very common precursors. The conflicts that precipitate suicidal acts are usually those that other people manage to live with. If they were so crucial, more people should be attempting suicide, and they don't.

ADW

In the absence of an overt attempt, it is useful to distinguish between suicide alert and suicide risk. Suicide is not a disease, nor is it an act of freedom. Suicide alert is a precaution like a forest fire alert during a dry spell. Suicide risk is a clinical judgment about how a patient will cope with prevailing problems. I must admit that I cannot tell you how to recognize the combustion point. Maybe we can use the seafaring analogy. Not every lifeboat will spring a leak and sink, but almost any boat can be caught in a storm and capsize. This is not a plug for fatalism. On the contrary, we evaluate each situation, repairing what we can, and then in a storm, hope to reach safe harbor.

Case 5. Multiple Suicide Attempts

ADW

We know that predicting suicide is difficult, but among various lethal factors, previous attempts and high intentionality are strongly associated with later attempts and higher risk/rescue ratings.

The patient was forty-five years old, unemployed, married, and the father of one son. He had used alcohol excessively for about five years, and was arrested for operating a motor vehicle under the influence on six occasions. We can infer that alcohol abuse and driving to endanger meant that self-destructiveness or destructiveness of others played a part in his clinical record. He also attempted suicide four times during the past five years.

JPL

Social service information comes to us from the patient's wife, a former nurse, and from his extensive hospital record. His mother, brothers, and sisters all refused to see me. Have you noticed how often significant others refuse to participate when we investigate a suicidal patient?

Many facts are available, so I'll just select those

which seem relevant. About five years ago, he began to increase alcohol intake. From a moderate social drinker he became a daily, round-the-clock drinker. He argued with his boss and parish priest. As a result, he stopped going to church, and was also fired from his job. Until then, he had been very conscientious about work and attending church. He went for many job interviews, but often showed up disheveled and smelling of alcohol. Finally, he stopped going to employment agencies and found a reason for not following up on job leads. He was afraid of failing again.

His mother is an important person in his life, a significant key other, I think, because her support meant the difference between life and death, or at least, how well or how badly he got along. She is described as a strong woman, who was widowed when our patient was seventeen. She supported a large family by running a rooming house and investing earnings in other real estate. At a time when our patient could not find work, she opened a liquor store and hired him as the manager, a gesture which seems to be of doubtful wisdom. When this didn't work out, she bought a small restaurant for him. This, too, failed, just three months before his first suicide attempt five months ago.

ADW

I thought his first attempt was five years ago.

JPL

No, his alcoholism and unemployment started five years ago. No suicide attempts until recently.

The chronology is this: Eight months ago, he opened the restaurant. It never succeeded, failing after three months. It was then that he attempted suicide for the first time, five months ago. Clear?

FGG

He has an extensive medical and surgical history, with many hospitalizations. At age three, poliomyelitis, without paralysis. At age eight, acute rheumatic fever. At age twelve, appendectomy. At age sixteen, he was found to have congenital polyposis of the colon. He was hospitalized at least sixteen times subsequently, including operations for bowel resection, and at age twenty-four, sympathectomy, because of cardiac hypertrophy and hypertension. At age twenty-nine, a resection of the aorta was performed because of coarctation.

Naturally, he was well known in the hospital, and earned a reputation for courage and stoicism. He even joked about his many illnesses, and endured every operation and hospitalization uncomplainingly.

He worked during the intervals between hospitalizations. At age thirty-one, he married a nurse, and had his only child, a son, six years later. All seemed well until five years ago.

As I got the story from him, he did not argue with the boss until his job required that he move to another part of the country. During his absence, his wife became ill after a miscarriage. He could not leave work to be with her, even when she subsequently had a hysterectomy. He was anxious and lonely, began to drink more and more, and finally gave up his managerial job to be with his family. So from his viewpoint, the alcohol intake increased while he was away, working and worrying about the health of his wife and one-year-old son. This version was not shared by his wife, who also reported that the family had to be supported by her and by his mother's contributions. With this background, uncertain though it is, let me describe the four suicide attempts.

No. 1. He is very discouraged about the failure of the restaurant. He sits at home, drinking, not bothering to open that day, until his wife becomes so exasperated that they quarrel again. Incidentally, she had given up her nursing job to be a waitress in this restaurant. She orders him out of the house. He leaves, goes to a park, sits, and broods. In the early evening, he goes to the restaurant, lets himself in, but does not open for business. He turns on the gas in the kitchen ovens, lies down, expecting to die.

An odd "coincidence" then happens. His sister and nephew drive by, something they had not done before. Now, I don't think for a moment that this visit was accidental. He could well have given them a signal about his despair. At any rate, they saw that the place was dark, and stopped. His nephew jimmied the door and found the patient on the floor of the kitchen. He was not unconscious, and after a brief conversation—I don't know what about—he was allowed to go home by himself, as if he had merely sobered up. Nothing changed during the next two months. He closed the restaurant, and did not work in any capacity. His wife finally persuaded him to consult a practitioner in the neighborhood about his drinking habits. Nothing was said about the suicide attempt.

No. 2. He talked with the doctor briefly, complaining about his sleeplessness and alcohol intake. He was given a prescription for secobarbital, which he filled, went home, and ingested the contents of the bottle. I don't know how much. When his wife returned home, he was comatose. Assuming that he had again passed out from drinking, she let him sleep. Hours later, however, he awoke, and told her what he'd done.

No. 3. Two months later he had another job interview, which like the others, failed. It suddenly occurred to him that he ought (sic!) to asphyxiate himself. He bought some garden hose, drove to a nearby, busy shopping center that his wife frequented, hooked up the hose to the exhaust pipe, and got into the back seat. Obviously, it was a crude job. Outside air mixed with the exhaust and he had to keep the car window partially open. Once again, his wife just happened to visit the shopping center, saw their car, and discovered him, not unconscious.

No. 4. One week later, he used the same method but went to another shopping center. This time, he was discovered by a local police officer who knew him from previous arrests. The officer took him to a local state hospital. Seven days later, he had a seizure, presumably related to alcohol withdrawal.

With this record, I expected to find a somewhat deteriorated man. I was surprised to meet a hale and hearty, jocular, and very verbose, overweight man who seemed on top of things. He minimized everything, and talked knowingly about other patients on the psychiatric ward. In a way, he was on home grounds, back in the hospital where he was well known and highly respected.

Note the many lethality factors, which contrasted with his hearty facade: chronic alcoholism, unemployment, history of hopelessness, many physical illnesses, arrests, threatened loss of a significant other (his wife was about to leave him), and four suicide attempts. It wasn't hard to interview him. He talked incessantly, presenting himself in the best possible light, but wasn't panicky in any sense. "Just call me Big Mike," he said, "Everyone else does." He told me how he advises his brothers and sisters, and slid over the five-year history of arrests, alcoholism, and so forth by giving me the facts without much detail.

LCJ

He may have been Big Mike to everyone, but on psychological testing, he came through like Little Joe.

The major theme in his TAT stories was extreme dependency and passivity with respect to his mother. One example. A son has been living in another city. Because of some tragedy, maybe a death, he comes home. Mother and son love each other deeply. She won't let him down. She will cook something good, and soon he'll feel better.

The Rorschach showed some puzzling anatomical responses. I wondered if they were related to his many operations or to his destructiveness, which he holds inside with his hearty amiability. Aggression was found everywhere. He talked about women who attempt suicide, not men, a response that raises a question of sexual identity. Other cards elicited ambiguous stories about which sex a person belongs to.

FGG

This matches my clinical impression. His cockiness, yes, that's the word, was like a child's. Do things my way, or not at all. From his wife's story, this behavior may be like his mother's. But then again, she might not be objective. Why the contrast, why the change over the past five years? One might say that after recovering from so many illnesses and operations, he worked very well until his success prompted his boss to put him in charge of a plant in another part of the country. Then he failed, began to drink, and felt lonely and hopeless when he couldn't be with his sick wife. If this version is true, it is a good example of "those wrecked by success." On the other hand, failure didn't seem to do very much for him, either.

HSO

Remember that this patient did much better in the hospital than on the outside. Although things began to worsen five years ago, he didn't attempt suicide until five months ago. Apparently, he had about ten years of comparatively good health, drinking a little, but working regularly, without complaints.

JPL

His wife told me that after his return he demanded an unreasonable pay raise from his boss, and when turned down, quit in a huff. He also split with the priest.

HSO

Oh, then he was on his own in a way, although his wife and mother continued to give him support. Maybe he needed a male in authority to keep him straight, and couldn't take his own initiative in any way. He was Big Mike, but needed to have a man over him. I surmise however that he antagonized prospective employers by his pseudoarrogance.

RSS

Let's look at him as a layman might. He is an oversized, self-centered child who expects too much, wants everyone to look after him, drinks too much, and can't hold a job. He's a mama's boy who grew up thinking that his illnesses give him a right to be cared for indefinitely.

Even his suicide attempts look like badly planned bids to be taken care of.

JPL

He was the advice giver on the outside, he claimed, not the help receiver. Why did this mother set him up for failure? Was it a mother's legendary blindness to her son's shortcomings, or did she want to keep him dependent? The family treated his drinking habits and arrests very lightly, I was told, but then several other men in the family had been in jail.

JWW

Obviously, we don't know why he went downhill five years ago, and began to attempt suicide five months ago. But let's look at some lethality factors.

According to the Risk-Rescue Rating, which measures the lethality of the implementation itself, all four attempts fall into the low moderate group. Our numerical values, given by a formula, divide attempts into high, high moderate, low moderate, and low lethality.

Clinically, however, we would have to consider him to be somewhat more lethal. He is a male over forty-five, with a history of medical/surgical illnesses, alcoholism, unemployment, recent disruptions with significant others, and progressive alienation.

A very useful clinical instrument has been described by Jan Fawcett for patients who are depressed and attempt suicide. He elicited ten factors in these patients which he thinks have predictive significance. These are (1) lifelong inability to maintain warm relationships (many people would call this "lack of mutuality"), (2) long-standing marital discord (disrupted relation with a significant other), (3) denial of dependence (pseudoautonomy), (4) negation of help (repudiation of help vs. cry for help), (5) hopelessness about positive change (typical of severe depression, a symptom usually called, simply, "hopelessness"), (6) failure to communicate intent, except to a significant other (I would think it is more ominous when a person fails to signal intent especially to a significant other), (7) attempt to please by conformity (this means placation, without true conviction), (8) wanting to die (which probably also includes wanting to be killed or to kill), (9) a history of psychosis (which probably indicates a tendency toward easy regression and defective reality testing), and (10) paranoid features (possibly this means that the person shows projection as well as depression, a combination that could add up to feeling overwhelmed by insurmountable forces). Note the absence of a factor called "feelings of guilt." I suspect that guilt is typical of severe depressions, but not discriminatory for people who also attempt suicide.

Anyway, this man is in Fawcett's high moderate

range of suicide riskiness. Because he has not, to our knowledge, been paranoid or psychotic, and speaks with some degree of hope for the future, he would not be scored as highly lethal. I could go into other kinds of lethality scales, but I think he would be in the moderate group according to any test.

RSS

Where is this man heading? He has a guarded prognosis.

JWW

According to our Index of Vulnerability, he is in the high moderate range. As you know, this instrument provides for rating hopelessness, perturbation, frustration, despondency, helplessness, anxiety, exhaustion, self-rebuke, painful isolation, denial, truculence and suspicion, repudiation of significant others, and time perspective (open or closed). Now, if we count in the multiple attempts as tangible evidence of suicidal coping strategies, plus his alcoholism and life-threatening–life-endangering behavior, he is very vulnerable. The veneer of self-confidence must be rated as an unfavorable sign. But, as we know, there are no instruments, psychological or physical, which measure when another attempt will be made. When RSS and I studied multiple attempters, we found that the older a person is when he enters the suicide-life, the more likely he is to make a high or moderately high attempt. The next attempt may be lower in lethality, but attempts later on will tend to be higher, i.e., more dangerous, than for those patients who begin with low lethality attempts. However, regardless of estimated lethality, it is possible for such patients to go for years without another attempt.

ADW

Can psychotherapy or other treatment modalities change the expectation?

JWW

We really don't know. But for a small sample, those with a history of psychiatric treatment show a greater length of time between attempts, and what is more important, subsequent attempts show a lower level of lethality, as measured by the Risk-Rescue Rating.

Case 6. Suicide and Cancer

ADW

In the public's mind, the very word *cancer* terrifies people. It is thought of as the prototype of fatal illness, conjuring up hopeless, painful, and debilitating disease. As professionals, we know that this is not true. However, if cancer has this reputation—and it does—it is possible that some people may contemplate or carry out suididal acts as a means of coping with the threat and reality of incurable illness.

Some experienced cancer physicians claim that suicide is rare. Other studies suggest that suicide attempts and cancer are not so infrequent. The fact is that there are few facts. But it is reasonable to believe that cancer, like other chronic illnesses, creates psychosocial problems, and that some patients, facing an uncertain or grim future, opt to terminate life. Today's patient attempted suicide under just such circumstances.

FGG

I am not going to give many details about this patient's physical status, except as it helps to localize psychosocial changes.

First, her present illness. Shortly after the birth of her seventh child, the patient, a thirty-four-year-old housewife, began to lose weight rapidly and to suffer severe abdominal pain. She postponed seeing a doctor for about six months. Then she was treated symptomatically for another three months. Finally, she came to this hospital, where a definitive diagnosis of adenocarcinoma of the stomach was made. Total gastrectomy was performed, but the prognosis was extremely poor. She had several admissions to the hospital afterward.

During the first admission, her husband was advised of the diagnosis and outlook. He insisted that his wife not be told. The surgeon, a very devoted doctor, agreed. Two weeks after the gastrectomy, she was discharged to her home. One month later, she was readmitted, with symptoms of partial obstruction. Her husband relented somewhat by telling his wife about the diagnosis, but still suggested that the outlook was favorable.

This kind of communication is not uncommon, either by family members or by physicians. A patient may be told that a "tumor" was discovered, but that it was removed. This encourages a patient to believe that the tumor—"cancer" is not used as often—is gone, although subsequent treatment and observation are recommended. It is a good example of second-order denial: knowing the diagnosis, but denying that other symptoms are related to the primary disease.

When the patient was discharged a second time, she

returned home again. The family then seemed to undergo a remarkable transformation, which she found more distressing than helpful. You see, she and her husband had always had a rather stormy, but basically compatible marriage. As we'll hear, they lived together several years before marrying, and she had children before that. They argued, sometimes fought physically, but stuck together. Now, after the diagnosis and poor prognosis became certain, he changed, becoming more considerate, less irascible, more helpful and sympathetic to her complaints. Neighbors and friends called on her more often. Even members of her family, whom she had not seen for several years, showed up and offered to help out. One of her brothers even presented her with new furniture for their modest house. These events were more puzzling than pleasing. She was accustomed to a constant tension at home, with many arguments and name-calling. People were different. She became suspicious, and concocted a story that her husband was having an affair with a neighbor woman to explain their sudden change of manner. As for herself, she believed that the profound weight loss, disability, sickness, and surgical scar had turned her into a "worthless freak."

Three weeks after her second hospital discharge, she overdosed with chlordiazepoxide (Librium) after drinking an unspecified amount of alcohol. No special treatment was administered for this first attempt, aside from observation in the emergency ward of a local hospital. Several days later, however, she overdosed again, taking seventy tablets of chlordiazepoxide, along with some amitriptyline (Elavil). Apparently, she had been given antidepressants and tranquilizers at an earlier time, but not in this hospital. She had not mentioned consulting anyone else. We also learned that since the gastrectomy she consumed much more alcohol than before, even though she knew it was forbidden. I call this an example of life-threatening behavior.

She was admitted to our psychiatric service after the second attempt. It was her third admission to this hospital. At this time, I became acquainted with the patient, and found out that on the day of the most recent attempt, she had been needling her husband about his good behavior. Fed up with her accusations and his own unaccustomed silence, he finally blurted out that if it made her feel any better, he'd get a divorce. This declaration made her feel that all the suspicions were correct. He was about to leave her.

JPL

For about two months, while she was on the psychiatric service, the patient refused to let any social worker talk with her family. No reason was given, but obviously, there was much to conceal. Finally she relented, especially when her husband came in to participate in some family activities.

Briefly, her father died when she was aged three. Her mother was said to be promiscuous, selfish, indifferent to any of her children. Social agencies supported the family for years, a fact which might have fostered her reticence about being interviewed.

When she was aged fifteen, she became pregnant. Her mother forced her to marry the sixteen-year-old father. She lived with him for about three years, then ran away, leaving two small children behind.

We are unclear about the next three years, from ages eighteen to twenty-one, except that her brother and sister finally found her living in a part of the city inhabited by drunks, addicts, low-class prostitutes, and derelicts. They brought her home, and shortly afterward she met the man she later married. The first two children had been placed for adoption. She had five other children by her present husband.

FGG

She improved considerably while on the psychiatric service, and strangely enough, had few physical symptoms. It wasn't surprising that she claimed to be almost cured of the cancer, but it was contrary to fact. One day, during a tense group session, she burst out, "None of you even tries to help yourself. If you had a death sentence hanging over you, maybe you'd get down to work and do something!" We weren't sure what she was suggesting by this remark, except that it exposed her awareness of encroaching death.

We had our doubts about her suicide risk. Although she seemed pretty well, she was just too impulsive, erratic, and truculently suspicious of the attention she got. In a word, the ward was just like her home.

Now it's time to mention another set of forces which got us into a collision course. Our project interest seemed to collide with that of the ward. The patient was also being seen by a ward psychiatrist and social worker. We should have conferred, but didn't. Maybe it had something to do with her third suicide attempt. She had been asking for a weekend leave of absence to attend a family christening. The staff reluctantly agreed; compassion overcame clinical judgment. She went to the christening, drank too much, argued with her mother, and then left in a huff with her husband.

She argued with him on the street as they walked home. When she reached a busy intersection, she suddenly jumped in front of an oncoming car. The alert driver slammed on his brakes, and she was not struck. The driver got out. Her husband was terrified, and shouted at him, "Get the hell out of here—my wife is a sick woman." Evidently he expected to be challenged by the driver, because he hit the man. While this was going on, our patient ran home and took more pills. It was an impulsive, low-lethality attempt, but in short succession, she made two life-threatening actions, which for our purposes, will be considered as a single attempt.

IP-1

I was part of the other set of forces that collided. Perhaps it is not fortuitous that Dr. FGG talked about the almost-collision that our patient precipitated on the street, after speaking about our almost-collision on the psychiatric ward.

I was the patient's psychiatrist who looked after her, with the help of our social worker. We followed the patient and her family even after discharge, until she died. The patient complained about your investigators, saying that they probed too much, and wished they would leave her alone. I could list her many objections, but in brief, she disliked your project workers intensely. . . .

FGG

This is very frustrating to hear about, and almost as surprising. I grant that we might have talked together. But we gave a lot to this patient, and at no time did I think that she objected to our attention, even though we were investigating suicide and cancer. The family, too, was cordial, at least for them. Now that I check back, they were friendly even at those times when the ward doctor says we were most unwelcome. Do I detect more animosity from the therapeutic team—the psychiatrist and social worker—than from the patient and her family?

I realize from this distance that we underestimated how our patient could split up people into good guys and bad guys. But I also think that the ward team has externalized its sense of competition and foisted it onto the patient.

She could play "End Game" very effectively. She did it with her husband and the fancied affair. She did it with us, fomenting guilt, frustration, and dissension between players other than herself.

The surgeon also was involved. I don't know if you knew that or not. Maybe you were too busy.

ADW

Easy, now. Let's just examine the facts.

FGG

Remember that at first the family relied completely on the surgeon, who complied with her husband's request and didn't tell her the diagnosis. Later, however, they both complained that he had misled them by pretending that the prognosis was better than it actually was. I have heard that to this day the surgeon feels that our project interfered with his management of the patient—an unfortunate thing because he is a very capable and compassionate man.

JPL

She told me how much benefit she got from her psychiatric stay, but then later on said that she'd rather die than be in a "mental hospital" again—a complete distortion, because our ward is not a mental hospital.

FGG

She seemed to think about the cancer in the same way she did about relationships in general. The world was out to get her, to belittle and humiliate her. So she shifted the blame onto others, belittling efforts to help which, face to face, she readily accepted. She turned people against one another—and I am reminded of the two children she abandoned and never spoke about. I guess I'm pretty angry at her, too.

IP-2

I don't know about that, but she was certainly angry at you and JPL. She didn't talk about death to us, but did say that you two were trying to force her to look at the most painful subject you could think of—death. Maybe she liked us because we didn't force her to do anything. We simply accepted the family as they were. We even gave the children presents at Christmas time.

JPL

Neither FGG nor I forced her to talk about death. Look how long I waited for her to give permission to interview her husband.

FGG

I can document that in my dictated interviews: whenever the topic of death comes up, it is the patient who mentions it! As a general policy, we don't initiate specific talk about death, though we don't back away from it, either. This is a distortion on her part, a version of the End Game. And you two seemed to have taken the bait.

[*More discussion of the failure to communicate, unraveling distortions, clarification of the problems.*]

IP-1

I can see now that we did tend to take her statements and complaints at face value, without realizing how she could split her ambivalence toward us. It's not unusual, I know, for people to antagonize someone they're afraid of losing. This happened with her husband, I can see, and perhaps to all of us.

FGG

She evidently devalued one person and praised the other, then reversed herself to prevent desertion.

HSO

This whole controversy could have been avoided. Why didn't you check with each other? It's common clinical practice, even plain common sense. When a patient tells us she can't stand another doctor, we ask if she has taken it up with him, and why not?

LCJ

She didn't fight directly with the two teams, but split them up. Perhaps this contributed to your not talking together; she got to you and made her position more solid.

ADW

I think Osler said that one should never believe what a patient tells you about another doctor, even if it's true. End Game, certainly. These were pretty rough people, not inclined to be very subtle, tactful, or devious, especially if things made them angry. I am trying to say that they probably couldn't contain ambivalence, anyway, and found it easier just to express it openly. But they did depend on the doctors, so they couldn't afford to antagonize them directly. They could do it with members of their family.

* * *

I'm afraid time has crept ahead with all our bickering about bickering. We haven't talked about the relation of suicide and cancer, and still haven't heard about her psychological testing.

JWW

I'll just hit the main themes.

She uses repression and denial predominantly, as shown by low productivity and blocking at key points. Her self-perception is that she is enmeshed in a topsy-turvy world. She is forced (note the frequency with which words like *force* and *being forced* come up) to deal with ill-defined, amorphous situations with unfamiliar, awkward strategies. Perhaps this has something to do with the suppression of impulses that the ward requires. Anyway, activity is her primary defense and coping strategy, even if the problem is not clear. She can handle only very simple problems in simple ways—no sophistication, no self-correction. With increasing disability, and with a diagnosis she could neither fight nor flee from, she externalizes her inner turmoil and foments fights.

I found mounting helplessness, confusion, fear of disorganization in her responses. I surmise that to some extent she helped to reduce and drain off her tensions and fears by using alcohol and by angry outbursts. There are no organic signs in her tests, as could show up if she suffered from cerebral metastases. Uncertainty prevails. Every TAT card but one refers to being lost and alone. She oversimplifies, then, if pressed, becomes confused. On a suicide card, 3 BM, in which a figure is seated on the floor, head hidden, with an object that looks like a revolver lying nearby: to her, this was a boy who had been drinking too much, and didn't know how to get to the bathroom. But things will be all right because he'll vomit and won't remember anything later, anyhow. Her guiding motto seems to be put the blame elsewhere—fight or drink, then forget it. The worst thing that could happen is to be ugly, deformed, and unwanted—all things she enacted in her dealings with us. She would like most to be—a dog. Dogs are friendly, and get a lot of attention. Least of all, she would be a rat. They're no good to anyone. They bite, are mad at the world, and carry disease that can kill you.

HSO

What about the suicide attempts and the cancer? Evidently, this group thinks that her ambivalence split off enough hostility and destructiveness to turn against herself. But she couldn't accept their considerate behavior toward her, and felt better when she bickered with her husband, fought with her mother.

I would guess that she attempted suicide after the

cancer operation when she decided that weight loss, scars, and symptoms of obstruction had turned her into a freak, deformed and disgusting.

ADW

Just a few words about the general connection between suicide and cancer. There are many possible correlations, ranging from none at all—simple co-incidence—to specific desires to end life, with its insurmountable problems. It is not a common event. Suicide is not common, but there are undoubtedly more cases than are recognized. A cancer patient who is found dead with an empty bottle at the bedside would probably not be signed out as a suicide. On the other hand, patients who attempt suicide seldom have concomitant cancer. I suspect that this patient is more typical than we realize, because there were intervening variables, such as gross self-loathing, fears of alienation and abandonment, and readiness to regress into impulsive, destructive behavior. She would score pretty high on the Index of Vulnerability; not so high, if we used Fawcett's factors. To generalize a little, I think that suicide and cancer can occur together if the threat created by the cancer causes deep fears of dissolution, disintegration, and drastic changes in social roles. Social dissonance seems more important than do physical disfigurement and deterioration. After all, hope is a function of self-esteem; hopelessness means that one is unable to recognize or to cope with insistent problems. Therefore, I would not expect much correlation between cancer stages and the time at which a suicide attempt is made. But I would expect considerable vulnerability, especially with a past history of lethal behavior.

FGG

Eight months after the first operation, the patient died at home. She and her husband had resumed their habitual bickering, shouting at each other and at their children, ordering them to behave. I think she accepted her fate; the family remained quite supportive, and in the last two months of life, there was no further talk or action about either suicide or insanity.

Case 7. Suicide and Organ Transplant

ADW

Organ transplantation is one of the great achievements of modern medicine. However, with each medical advance there are new problems. The price of progress may be that people are saved from one fatal disease only to die of others. Certainly this is true with organ transplantation. In preventing tissue rejection, infections may be ignited, healing delayed, neoplasms initiated. Patients become exceedingly vulnerable—psychologically as well as physically—to what would ordinarily be minor injuries.

Only the kidney has been transplanted often enough to offer a feasible procedure for large groups within the population. Here, too, survival itself imposes many secondary problems. Extension of life does not necessarily restore the quality of life. Renal dialysis patients may choose to discontinue the program because they are so hampered by the narrow range of options available to them. In a sense, they elect death rather than unrelieved dependency. Kidney transplants that are technically successful may create emotional and social disasters, and when repeated transplants fail, patients may give up entirely. The case today will not settle anything, but it will show what happens to some people who undergo this procedure.

HSO

Kidney patients usually have a very extensive medical history. This man was no exception, so I will confine myself to a brief account of the major events. Then we'll hear from the head nurse and social worker on the Kidney Transplant Unit staff.

This man first developed progressive kidney disease at age nineteen, and finally succumbed at age forty-one—a span of time that consumed about half his lifetime. He was a fisherman, like the rest of his family. They all lived on a common tract of land in northern Maine. But they shared more than a common occupation and residence. He was the third youngest of twelve siblings, and learned from earliest childhood to share property and to maintain staunch family loyalty. During one of his few remissions, he started to build a fishing boat for the family. He relapsed again before it could be completed. The unfinished boat still stands on family property, a mute symbol of an unfinished life, but a life of devotion and loyalty to their common aim.

He was first admitted here ten years ago, when he was aged thirty-one. Six years ago, he had the first kidney transplant, with his brother as donor. It was rejected fourteen months later. Then a second transplant, with his sister as donor, was performed, but this, too, was rejected. A third transplant from an anonymous nine-year-old was carried out about a year ago. But let's hear from the social worker.

IP-1

I knew the patient and his wife very well, following them for a long time. He was a stolid and agreeable man, who always went along with family decisions. His wife said that she had seen him angry only once during their eighteen-year marriage. He was diligent, hardworking when his health allowed, and was very unhappy whenever he was away from home.

I'd like to concentrate on the events of the past year, after the third transplant. In addition to an endless series of medical complications, he lost his father through a heart attack, a brother, an aunt, and a sister. His mother died of diabetes twenty years ago. These losses evidently were contributing factors because when admitted to the hospital for a checkup, he was obviously depressed, and no longer the stoical man I had expected.

IP-2

I have been the head nurse on the unit, and know the patient, his wife, children, and some members of his family. When he returned after the third transplant, he was not only depressed, but complaining (he never complained very vociferously) of failing vision. This was attributed to diabetes, a complicating disease of therapy.

Even during the years of dialysis, he was quietly optimistic, even though it was difficult for him to be away from home. It was a happy day for all when he was first selected for a transplant. In the months that followed, he returned regularly for checkups, always bringing us boxes of clams and lobsters. Then the rejection process commenced. He had to be hospitalized again and again in futile efforts to save the kidney. Later, he was again hospitalized for the second transplant. This lasted for a couple of years. About a year ago, however, he began to fail. Vision and diabetes worsened. He developed a testicular abscess which resisted antibiotics, and the testis finally had to be removed. There were numerous infections at various sites, which healed with great difficulty, if at all. I do remember one hospitalization in which both the patient and the entire staff were very depressed and discouraged. After he went home, I happened to be driving through his town and stopped to visit. He was remarkably improved in spirits, showing that just being at home helped.

We were all very pessimistic, but went ahead with a third transplant. I suppose this is the focal event that Dr. HSO will describe.

HSO

There are a number of events which could be called "focal." On the occasion just mentioned, on another later on, and on a still later occasion. For present purposes, however, I'll cite a forerunner and then the focal event of a suicide attempt.

In the early spring, when fishing industry flourishes, [our man] must return to the hospital once more. The testicle has been removed, but the abscess persists. Diabetes is difficult to control, and his vision diminishes.

One night he simply asks the nurse to remove the scissors from the room because he is afraid of what might happen. The following day he asks his wife not to let him be alone with the children. No reason is given because she assumes that he does not want his children to see him crying, as he had.

Several months later, he is admitted again, suffering with recurrent infections, pneumonia, and anginal attacks. It is the middle of the week, and the only unusual event is that he is to have a leave-of-absence for the next weekend, so that he can stay with his wife and children in a small apartment they had rented near the hospital. He has an arteriovenous shunt in his arm. Earlier in the day, several sutures from his back were removed, but a furuncle persists, causing some pain. Nothing else is noted until that night, shortly after midnight. The nurse on duty makes her rounds, goes into his room and finds the patient engulfed in blood, his rubber shunt cleanly cut.

I saw him within two hours, but of course, emergency measures had started before that. He lost about five units of blood, and was sedated. When I was able to talk with him on the following morning, he was amnesic, but said that he must have cut the shunt, although he couldn't recall. His wife did report that he had said she'd be better off without him. Evidently, this was not an unusual statement because she didn't tell anyone.

What I want to ask this group is why *now* does he make a suicide attempt. He was desperate, discouraged, preterminal, I suppose, but still . . . twelve years of hospitalization, including ten years of repeated admissions here . . . why?

ADW

When we don't know how to answer a question, we usually turn it back on the questioner. What do you think?

HSO

Well . . . he was steadily getting worse, deteriorating in every respect. His quiet optimism was gone; mental problems and physical disabilities were multiplying. He was not only depressed, but intermittently confused. Even the mildest, most sedentary work was out of the question, due to his angina and his failing vision. He couldn't carry out any life-threatening behavior, because he always complied with what was expected of him. He did give a signal to the nurse and his wife about the scissors. I think that cutting the shunt was the only effort of which he was capable, and it meant severing his link to the hospital, as well. He didn't want his children to see him so depressed before, and with the forthcoming weekend, this could have been decisive so far as ending his life.

ADW

I don't suppose any of us could elaborate on that.

HSO

You must realize that patients on the Kidney Unit usually enter with great expectations. Not only do they regard transplantation as a miraculous reprieve that just wasn't available a few years ago, but they have been selected. They are reprieved both from certain death and from the restrictions of a dialysis existence. Transplantation is a kind of miracle. It is not unreasonable for some patients to ignore the risks, failure, or rejection, and to anticipate returning to a full and effective life. For most patients—statistics bear me out—this will be a futile hope. They don't find their independence restored. Their survival may be stretched out, but at a price of more sickness than they ever imagined enduring. It is one thing to talk about hope, but something else to keep hope or even a little courage alive, when everything else is falling to pieces. For this man, only bitter fragments. I come back to the half-built boat which will never sail. He, too, will never fish, perhaps never see or walk by the sea again.

He had little to lose by suicide. He was also ashamed of his failures. By this I mean two kinds of failure: failure as a family member, husband, and father, and the failure of the two transplants. His brother and sister had forfeited their kidneys on his behalf and to no avail.

RSS

Were these donors the ones who died during the past year?

HSO

No, they were other siblings. But let's not get away from my question, why now?

FGG

I can see that his periodic confusion, helped along by sickness and visual problems, could create a quiet delirium. At least, his retrospective amnesia after the attempt is consistent with this. We know that in delirium patients may quickly forget their hallucinatory experiences, like a bad dream, or like a tape that is erased as soon as it is played.

IP-2

I mentioned that all of us were very discouraged, and this might have been conveyed to him. And he did get a lot of drugs. He was in a kind of stupor much of the time. I agree that he, like others, expected miracles, but by now, he knew that this wasn't the place where miracles would be performed. He wanted to be home, not at the apartment.

LCJ

It sounds as if he felt he'd let everyone down, doctors and nurses, as well as his family. A lot had been invested.

JWW

I did some psychological tests with him after the attempt, not before, and the circumstances were far from ideal. His answers were brief. The TAT outcomes were either very tentative, or had no outcome at all. The word *probably* prefaced everything he said. It indicated a rather detached and impersonal approach, not a closely analytic qualification.

He would prefer being a dog, because they're taken care of and lead an easy life. But—this is strange—he couldn't think of any animal that he would prefer not being. It was as if any animal were better off than he. I found no sign of further suicidal ideation.

One week later, testing him with the POMS, his tension was high; he was scored as low on anger, but moderately high on depression and quite confused—not confused enough, however, because he did carry out the test, which is self-administered. He was ashamed of the suicide attempt, and didn't want to discuss it further.

ADW

What about the future for this man? He went home again, didn't he?

IP-1

We don't have to speculate. He did go home, didn't improve. Over the next seven months he had two heart attacks which were treated in a local hospital. I kept in telephone touch with his wife, and learned that he said very little. Maybe he was just too sick, but no further suicide attempts were made. He also had a lot of intestinal ulceration. He had been out of the hospital for about two weeks, and was sitting on their porch, doing nothing in particular. When his wife brought lunch out to him, she found him dead.

HSO

By our silence, I see that we all empathize with this man's sense of futility. We have nothing to say. Perhaps we can respect his right to call it quits, and not to endure further illness and pain. His life was already over when he went home. He had further heart attacks, probably recurrent angina, and pain from the ulcerated intestines. At least he was at home. He could await death passively. Suicide was no longer an imperative.

Case 8. The Question of Appropriate Death

ADW

Most articles and conferences about death these days call attention to our society's tendency to deny the reality of death. Euphemisms about "going away," plastic rituals, and convenient escape hatches prevent people from confronting their own mortality. Death is what happens to someone else, not to us or to anyone close to us. On the other hand, we are also finding a tendency to glamorize death; it is the new chic topic. I notice that the people who find death so glamorous often forget that people are very sick before they die, that people may be killed in vastly brutal ways. Death as a new chic may mask the reality just as effectively as the older systematic denial we rail against.

I find it hard to imagine living in a society that would be wholly death-oriented, even though in the midst of life, we are in death. We couldn't live without repression; we couldn't perform without some degree of avoidance; and I suppose we couldn't understand without also denying a portion of reality. I believe that at the core of human existence there is ambiguity about what we know, ambivalence about what we feel, and anxiety about what we are. So I guess that we ought to become accustomed to ambiguity, ambivalence, and anxiety in our fluctuating attitudes toward death and dying.

We take it as an "axiomatic truism" that we want to live our own life. Since dying is a part of living, then we are obliged to die our own death. We can't complain about the taboos surrounding death. Our task is to understand how a person's characteristic life-style leads to a certain death-style. What is a "good death"? What kinds of death can we live with? Perhaps there are no ideal deaths, and I am reasonably sure that most people would prefer life over death. All of us fear something in dying and death. But die we must. Therefore, we want to know what kinds of death would be acceptable. Given a little choice and autonomy, what death would be best for us, the death most consistent with the values and aims we have followed throughout life?

The most commonly held view about death is that it is an evil, the most tragic event to befall anyone, the ultimate catastrophe. The other view, that death is chic or cool, is hardly better, although it does acknowledge the inevitability of death and the possibilities for coming to terms with our deepest anxieties. In either case, I suspect that dying people are avoided in one way or another.

People find it difficult to imagine extinction in a personal sense. The idea of death as evil stems from older notions about hellfire and damnation. The cool view may be an updated idea of death as eternal bliss. But speaking about modern versions of religious theories of death, what about the role of religion in caring for the dying? Certainly clergymen have had the central role for generations. Nowhere are we more aware of powers greater than our frail organism than on the threshold of death. But as a clinician I find the question very hard to formulate. Does "religion" refer to church membership, regular attendance at services, beliefs about life after death (incidentally, I believe in life before death), participation in ritualized practices derived from religion, or simply deep persuasion about man's value, dignity, and significance?

Lest you think that I am about to take up our psychological autopsy time today with a sermon about death, we are going to discuss a specific case. It is not necessarily a prototype appropriate death, but it does raise questions about our human obligation to die, about survival and the meaning of significant survival, and about becoming nothing at all. Perhaps these are the questions that religion is supposed to deal with.

Our patient was a reformed alcoholic who died of myeloblastic leukemia in middle age. During the years of heavy drinking, he had forfeited his family, his opportunities, his health. He had little to show for having lived, except that through Alcoholics Anonymous he had given up drinking, and helped to rescue others.

Alcoholics Anonymous is, of course, not an established church. But it does profess a series of principles that are couched in religious language—more importantly, AA requires that to be successful, one must practice these principles daily. In a psychosocial sense, therefore, successful AA members have adopted a sincere and quasi-religious orientation toward life and its goals. How does it affect their orientation toward death? Now I'll shut up.

JPL

Here is a brief social history.

Five years after undergoing a kind of conversion experience and becoming thenceforth a faithful adherent of AA, this patient developed the blood disease that ultimately claimed his life.

His father was born in Ireland. Until his marriage in his mid-twenties, he was a merchant seaman. We know little else except that he was subject to periodic depressions and to bouts of heavy drinking. He was treated here years ago for a nervous stomach and fear of syphilis. While our patient was overseas during World War II, his father either fell or jumped to his death from a nearby bridge.

Our patient's mother felt that she had married beneath herself socially, but their Catholicism kept them together without seeking a divorce. They fought frequently. Two brothers were alcoholics, and a sister was hospitalized after attempting suicide. Another brother died at age sixteen. After this tragedy, his mother turned away from the church. Our patient was his mother's favorite. He was bright, attractive, and the only one of his siblings to have advanced education. I assume that his life was supposed to justify his mother's. He attended a prestigious prep school, went to an Ivy League university, and at age twenty-eight, married the only daughter of a prominent attorney. The marriage did not go well. Two years later, at age thirty, he began to use alcohol excessively, but during this time, two daughters were born. At age thirty-three, he lost a good job. Thereafter, everything deteriorated. He and his wife split up frequently, only to resume living together for awhile. In the intervals he lived with his mother. His job was pumping gasoline, certainly beneath his education and capacity.

HSO

He was well-known to this hospital. At age thirty-four, when he was referred to our alcohol clinic, he denied that he had any drinking problem, even though he had already lost a good job. Nevertheless, for the next two years, he and his wife were seen regularly; he was treated by two competent psychiatrists (not at the same time!) and his wife had social work counseling. The consensus was that he was worth saving, if possible; so his diagnosis was depression, not psychopathy. Like so many others, the staff liked him.

Unfortunately, the results of therapy fell far far short of the abundant enthusiasm and effort expended by the staff. His wife divorced him and remarried within several months. He lived with his mother, with whom he argued. Finally, he dropped out of therapy altogether.

There are so many things that I could mention . . .

but here are a few high spots. He returned to the hospital several times for alcohol abuse and abusive behavior toward his ex-wife, and then his mother. He was admitted, but then signed out again. The hospital record always reports how charming, intelligent, likable, he is, then how he disrupts the psychiatric ward before signing out. He was never refused admission, a sign that the staff still found him bright and promising. Women in particular extended themselves in every possible way to help him through the years.

At age thirty-nine, he developed tuberculosis and was sent to a sanatarium. After several months, he had to be discharged for disciplinary reasons. Three more years elapsed. He came here again for cervical nerve root compression, but the main problems were alcoholism, tuberculosis, and, by this time, not only unemployment, but unemployability. One year later, he savagely beat his mother while intoxicated, and the police were called.

Now the focal event, or critical moment, call it what you wish.

He is now age forty-three, down and out. Early one morning he awakens to find himself lying in a doorway on Skid Row. He remembers nothing about how he got there. An empty wine bottle lies nearby and he knows that he finished it. Dazed and groggy, he gets up. The street is dirty and deserted. The sun is just coming up over the dilapidated buildings. He sees his own reflection in a store window—dirty, bedraggled, a real bum. As he stands there gazing into the window, he realizes how far he has fallen. He then goes to a police station, and asks to be put away, anywhere. The police oblige, and send him to an institution which is both psychiatric and penal. It is a very old place, used to confine incorrigible psychopaths. Professional staff is minimal. Nevertheless, he is contacted by a member of AA. The conversion takes. He is dry for the next five years until his death.

Now I'll skip ahead to the fatal illness—our focal event—which came five years later, give or take a few months. I saw him about ten times during hospitalization here. He had several courses of chemotherapy, but because of tuberculosis, he did not receive prednisone, which usually activates any latent infection. He was kept in isolation.

I remembered him from earlier admissions to the psychiatric service. Despite his illness, he was still a most charming and articulate man who engaged me in intelligent conversation, and seemed to show full knowledge of his plight. I expected people to be taken in by him, but I also thought that he'd be filled with denial—he wasn't. Without agitation, alarm, or bargaining, he simply accepted the situation.

In our sessions together, his major theme was Alcoholics Anonymous. If there ever was a convert, it was he. He refreshed my meager memory of the Twelve Steps, including the precept, *one day at a time.* He also spoke with regret about his mother, who died of cancer about a year before. His worry was that he, too, might have a painful course and would relapse into alcoholism, which he evidently dreaded more than death itself. He had a few visitors, a card from his daughters, and a couple of women came to call. But he gradually became more and more depressed, doubting that he'd ever leave the hospital and return to the small-time job he held.

About one month before his death (chemotherapy produced no improvement at this time) he asked to speak with me. He heard that AA met weekly in the hospital chapel, and wondered if I could arrange permission for him to attend. I cautioned him about his physical condition, and urged that he stay for only part of the meeting in case he became too tired. As it turned out, however, the meeting acted like a shot in the arm, or better, in his case. He was reenergized completely; the depression had gone by the time he came back to his room. Ten days later, he remained so well that he was discharged home. His home was a small apartment which he shared with a male friend. He was quite realistic about the future, but did not expect to die very soon. He was hopeful for a limited time perspective, to use our jargon.

LCJ

Before we go on, I'd like to report his psychological findings. He was straightforward, articulate, and enjoyed a chance to talk about himself and AA. He was not discouraged because of his belief in one day at a time. Ordinarily, we would interpret this as denial, or avoiding a problem by rising above it. Reality testing was intact. He knew that he had risen from Skid Row, and while he wasn't at the point of adolescent expectations, and didn't have very much going for him, his triumph over alcoholism was significant, and he knew it.

The POMS showed high vigor (not unusual for some bedridden, preterminal patients), low tension, low anger, low depression. The TAT was very productive. The Farm Scene was thought to express serenity, orderly habits, and acceptance of nature. He added a bit of doubt by saying that things are not always as neatly plowed and well-organized as they appear on the surface. This conveyed to me his deep misgivings about his own seeming order and control. Card 10, you remember, shows a couple embracing. He said that it represented peace, devotion, contentment, and security between a man and wife. But several other cards indicated feelings of hopelessness and ambiguity. Other cards were like a bad dream that was very depressing. I suspect that he had many bad dreams.

HSO

All right, let's go on to the terminal events. Recall that he was feeling well when discharged home; he even wondered about taking his meals somewhere else, and when his strength came back, he might return to work.

Within forty-eight hours, he was back, complaining of intense anxiety and profound weakness. He had gone to bed as soon as he reached the apartment. He awakened in a panic on the following morning, bombarded with persistent obsessional thoughts about being unable to take action on some unspecified task. He had no idea what this was, but it reminded him of his alcoholic years. Similar feelings would invariably lead to more and more drinking, just to calm himself. It was something he had to do, but didn't know what, except that he couldn't do it. That night, he went to an AA meeting. It helped. When he returned to his apartment he again felt very lonely and afraid that he would give up and start to drink again. He waited several more hours and then came back to the hospital, where he was found to have a fever of 104 degrees. He was desperately ill. In short, the remission ended as soon as he left the hospital premises. Now he was preterminal, at the very least. During the next few days he improved slightly. Ten days before death ($D-10$) he talked at length about his mother. On the $D-8$ day he asked for an AA representative because he felt too weak to attend the hospital sessions. His temperature zoomed to 106 degrees! On the $D-6$ day, a woman friend called, and he again asked about a room outside where he might stay and have meals brought to him. Note that despite the high fever he was clear, clear enough to demonstrate middle knowledge. But it also showed how afraid he was of being alone. He admitted to me that he would never leave the hospital, whether because of loneliness, fear of alcohol, or the illness could not be determined. The distinction was academic, anyway. On the $D-4$ day, he slipped into semistupor, asking if he were terminal. The doctor could only say, in honesty, that this was an expected part of his disease. Then, for about the first time, he showed some anger and wondered if he were being experimented on. The question does have a paranoid ring, but as I heard it in context, it seemed to reflect his helplessness about people who were not forthright with him. On the $D-2$ day, he asked again, and this time got a straight answer. He was still very much alone, and the floor nurses became upset and alarmed about his incipient death—as if they were his only family and only mourners. To prove this assumption, several weeks after his death, these nurses asked to meet with me to discuss their feelings about him. He wept from time to time during the next forty-eight hours. Yes, he didn't want to die; yes, he was a little afraid to die. Most of all, he wanted to be set free, to be at peace within himself. Again, he mentioned his dead mother, no one else. Then he fell silent, and within a few hours was dead.

JPL

Would you consider this an appropriate death?

ADW

I'm wondering if his "religion," AA, helped him toward the end. Let's try to piece things together; I'm trying to feel my way, too. Deciding that one death is appropriate and another not depends upon distinguishing between what would be appropriate for us and what would be appropriate for the other person. Step by step, now. Obviously, it was not an "ideal" death—I don't know what that would be. The death was expected by the patient and by the staff. It was untimely only in that he was still in middle years. But that was his life span or allotment, and we can't do much about that. He had a lot of support, from the staff, from HSO, and from AA. In his final hours, he wept, spoke about his mother, not about anyone else. His daughters evidently belonged to a life he had already lived. He was a little afraid of dying, but had been spared the pain he feared. One day at a time. On his brief stay outside the hospital he went into a panic, and presumably now was reconciled to staying in the hospital until death. He was less alone, I think, and far more alive than he had been on that morning when he awakened on Skid Row. That would certainly have been an anonymous, John Doe death. Conquering alcoholism was a genuine victory. Like so many of our terminal patients, psychosocial and physical problems seem to fuse. For him, alcoholism was always a threat; he was endangered from this and from his leukemia. And he was helpless in both instances.

HSO

The concept of appropriate death is still very elusive. Do you regard it as a fair approximation of a person's life-style, with minimal conflicts and suffering, or is it a developmental stage one transcends, becoming more or better than one was before?

ADW

I am only guessing. He did transcend what he was on Skid Row, and Skid Row was the nadir of his descent. He was no longer a derelict, but could put his considerable charm and attractiveness to use. This wasn't all, of course, because he rode the rail to hell by means of his charm and likableness. He was alcoholic to the end, as AA insists. One must recognize helplessness and the reality of a superior power, they say, but here the superior power was the disease as well as the deity. If life-style combines adaptive and innovative behavior, this man showed a capacity to live and belong in the world without overestimating his strengths or weaknesses. He was not a serene person. He was prone to violence in early times. His sister and possibly his father attempted suicide. He wasted much potential. But we should distinguish between a life that a man actually leads and the life we think he might have led, and was fated never to reach. His ego ideal was very simple: to be alcohol-free. He reached this.

JWW

Before we get carried too far into existential issues, Project Omega does have some operational questions to ask about appropriate death.

Answer these questions:

(1) Did he have adequate medical care and relief of pain toward the end of his life?
(2) How competently did he manage his life until he died?
(3) To what degree did he keep rewarding or significant relationships during the terminal period?
(4) Did he die with a decent self-image and a feeling of personal significance?
(5) Were there signs of conflict resolution?
(6) What about the "personal consent to die"—that he had nothing more to live for?

HSO

I guess you're right about ambiguity, ADW. But I'll try to answer JWW's questions. His only significant relationships were in the hospital and in Alcoholics Anonymous, two churches, you might say. They gave him very good support. He didn't have the usual family ties, occupational rewards, social values. Triumph over alcohol was about all he had, and he kept fighting the tendency to relapse. His fever spiked when his panic was at its height, too. Yes, he had adequate medical care, no pain, and a decent self-image. Consent to die? Not the serenity he saw and saw through in the TAT farm scene.

LCJ

He saw his frailty very clearly, and didn't offend us by pretending a false serenity toward the end. In my opinion, considering how AA emphasizes personal helplessness, yet personal responsibility, his self-image was pretty decent.

ADW

Let me refresh your knowledge of AA by paraphrasing their precepts (which I reviewed earlier this week!): (1) We must admit that our life is unmanageable. (2) Only a power greater than I can reduce my cravings and restore sanity. (3) We must decide to turn over our will and life to the care of God as we understand him. (4) We must make a fearless moral inventory, admitting our wrongs, and making amends, except when to do so would cause further injury to others. (5) Through daily prayer and meditation we improve our consciousness of contact with God, and ask only for knowledge of his will and for power to carry our task. If we do all this, then ours will be a spiritual awakening . . .

LCJ

This man did not restore any family life, and presumably he hadn't reconciled himself with his mother at the time of her death. Nevertheless, he shows how someone can be hopeless but not helpless, and still muster enough to be responsible.

ADW

Don't confuse the pigeon with our pigeonholes. What is appropriate for me may not be appropriate for you. Operational criteria for an appropriate death are all right, but what can they tell us about how to measure the meaning of death for any individual? The final judge is the patient—whether it feels right to die at that moment.

The key concepts of appropriate death are awareness, acceptability, resolution, relief, and these are the concepts used to characterize successful coping. We can deplore death, as we might deplore lots of other things we must accept. Must successful living and dying be based on the adversary system? Is death really a problem, or do we make it so? This man died his own death. He had a dignified demise. I think we can look back on him with deep respect, both as what he was and might have been. Well, enough for today.

Chapter 5

COMMON DENOMINATORS
OF DEATH

In Search of a System

How useful is the psychological autopsy? What are its problems, promises, and potential? Is a wider application of the method justified or feasible? Who will initiate, participate, and carry the burden of investigation?

We cannot doubt but that the current popularity of death and dying as subjects of seminars and articles will peak. We must also hope that mere reiteration of humanistic principles will be replaced by more systematic studies of death-related problems—if thanatology is to survive.

What is the next step? This guide for the psychological autopsy is only a partial answer. What follows is a more technical study of how we can move from philosophical precepts and clinical conditions into an operational definition of psychosocial forces, which then may help define coping, vulnerability, life-threatening behavior, as well as the factors in the observer that decide which perceptions are relevant and

153

what actions are desirable to improve and alleviate patients.

At this moment, the main function of the psychological autopsy is to gain a forum for the nonorganic factors in patients on or near the threshold of death. We use the organic evidence, gathered from the bedside, laboratory, and autopsy room. But we evaluate this evidence in the light of psychosocial information. Mutual discussion has merit. Scientific studies, however, demand systematic premortem and postmortem assessment. Without a system of sorts, however rudimentary, the psychological autopsy will operate in the dark, groping toward principles but lacking relevant form. The illustrative cases in the previous chapter provide a glimpse of how we must improve our questions in order to ask better questions, not to find definitive answers. The term, *system*, has many implications. It can be used as a slogan or a program. I use the term as a plea for more coherent concepts, coupled with specific methods of gathering information. Otherwise, one generation will simply perpetuate the doctrines and preconceptions of its predecessors, and that phase of life which confronts death will remain obscure and terrifying.

Psychiatric, psychological, and casework reporting is notoriously imprecise—and for good reasons. Human behavior is difficult to measure and to describe except in naturalistic language. Furthermore, we are pledged to confidentiality and the protection of privacy. From a purely investigative standpoint, interviews cannot be repeated; even another interview with the same patient by the same interviewer takes place under different circumstances and with different expectations by both participants. Reports usually must stand alone, their reliability unquestioned, but not unquestionable. Clinical anecdotes and dramatic episodes can be very compelling, and the individual psychiatrist, for example, can be very persuasive as he narrates a captivating story. As a rule, however, he reports only his conclusions; his information often is inadequate justification for his stylized presentations.

I exaggerate, of course, but it is still true that behavioral observations are more than just objective observations of behavior. They are also attributive summaries of motives, meaning, moods. Any case is only a "for instance," and may not even be typical of the patient's style of coping with problems. In the psychosocial domain, hard data are very hard to come by. The data we use may be simply how an observer selects his material, what appeals to him, what implicit theories about reality he uses.

It is easy to be content with keeping postmortem conferences at a conversational level. We learn from each other. By sharing our thoughts and feelings about a patient we can reach emotional closure as well as a degree of understanding. These experiences are rewarding, indeed, as most people who participate agree. It is by no means an exercise in futility to talk about the psychological and social surroundings of a patient who died or attempted suicide.

To venture beyond this into the realm of strategic and systematic investigation is both challenging and frustrating. It requires formulation of problems, development of tests for behavior that has not previously been specified, establishment of criteria and evidence. Throughout our investigation, we insist upon careful adjudication of conclusions, both in premortem interviews and postmortem interpretations. Although the case illustrations in the previous chapter simply presented samples of the autopsy at work, what was not explicit are the problems needing further formulation and investigation.

Guidelines for reasonably reliable and systematic study are determined by three criteria: *generality*, *specificity*, and *relevance*. It is difficult to achieve all three simultaneously. As a rule, we must compromise. The price of one or two is forfeit of the others. Therefore, our pursuit of system is often hampered by three common problems: overgeneralization from a few instances, compulsive precision, which sacrifices overall comprehension by scrupulous attention to minutiae, and irrelevant information, which may be measurable and self-evident, without being very informative.

Admittedly, we can only draw samples from the flow of material, and our methods of analysis are still so rudimentary that slanting is inevitable. Healthy skepticism is always needed, but we are familiar with the "empiricist" who doubts simply for the sake of challenging another person, without offering an alternative hypothesis. Obstinacy sometimes dons the guise of methodological sanctity, in the same way that private obsessions become "scientific" hypotheses.

Even though we operate out of inadequate foundations and limited knowledge, not every inference or generalization is fallacious. If we truly believed that our constructions were wholly guesswork, we could not work at all.

We interpret only what can be perceived. Often enough, we perceive only what we can interpret. This is not equivalent to perpetual subjectivity. An enlightened, inquiring attitude can concede its debt to intuition and irrationality, without yielding to the notion that psychological constructions might as well be misconstructions.

It is, of course, praiseworthy to be operational, but it is difficult to be sure what operations we use when we do so. Premature or fallacious objectivity in psychosocial matters may preclude further inquiry because we are eager to reach operational certainty. Our uncertainty, blended into reports, perceptions, and interpretations, can be biased unwittingly by our very skills as well as by our mistakes. Some of the common sources of bias are professional expertise, personal prejudice, selective inattention, and overgeneralization.

Professional expertise is an artifact of specialization. We need experts in every discipline to create new disciplines and subspecialties. However, specialists can create entities out of their own constructs and methods, populating a world that simply does not exist for living experience. If we imagine a revised version of the old tale about blind men and the elephant, let us say that instead of merely feeling different parts of the elephant, one man can see, but only see. Another man can feel, but only feel; another hears, but only hears; and so forth.

Then let us suppose there are experts in following elephant trails, and ivory specialists, and experts who specialize in the trees of the forest. And imagine, too, specialists in the language of elephants, say, zoo keepers who know by experience when elephants are hungry, sleepy, angry, depressed, or excited.

Why stop here? A zoologist might and would see the beast differently from a hunter on safari, searching for a trophy. In brief, each specialist constructs the entity, elephant, out of preexisting perceptions, interpretations, and expectations of what *elephants* are, might be, and how they ought to behave with respect to his own body of knowledge. Expertise has a professional circularity that prompts specialists to favor their own company, and to find mutual confirmation in diminishing diameters.

Unless we seek a common language of mutual experience and avoid specialized dialects, it will be impossible for the behavioral scientist, say, to agree upon interdisciplinary matters with a surgeon or a pastoral counselor or even with a nurse. We talk a common language, but except for a few transactions still may find it impossible to share a common reality.

Personal prejudice slants observations when events are interpreted according to private standards. For example, if we expect terminal patients to be depressed, then whatever we allow or perceive will be consistent with that judgment. If we expect a dying patient to be very apprehensive and afraid of death, and the patient displays none of the signs of anxiety as time runs out, then our personal prejudice will certainly decide that the patient denied fear until the very end. Prejudice by definition leads us to find whatever we are looking for, and then to insist that what we found is confirmation.

Our behavior is often a reflection of how we expect others to behave. If they do not conform to our standards of desirability, we are apt to be critical, and find ways of urging them to conform on other grounds. An angry patient, for example, is not always angry at us. He may be irritated and annoyed about his refractory course and persistent symptoms. We may return his anger anyway by becoming angry with him, because we expect patients to be appreciative, nonangry, and polite. But if we understood or interpreted manifest anger as a sign of dismay, not of destructiveness, the patient's behavior would be more tolerable, because we could reconcile his anger with our standards. Personal prejudice is not an all-or-none event; the assessment of motives and appraisal of personality depend upon broadening our base of perceptions and having access to other standards of desirable, expectable behavior.

Private prejudice can easily be detected if we look for value judgments in the observer's report. Discussions sprinkled with words like good/bad, right/wrong, strong/weak, realistic/neurotic, cooperative/negativistic are apt to be categorical surmises about a patient, without qualifying the observer's perceptions or allowing for individual differences. If we like a patient, we think he is "courageous," while another patient, behaving in a similar way, is thought to be "stubborn."

Selective inattention makes us alert to certain situations, oblivious to others, to underscore some statements as more typical than others, and to omit information that is inconsistent with what we already believe. It is undoubtedly the most difficult bias to detect during a psychological autopsy. Data must be condensed and explained at the same time. We like to make sense out of what we are told, remembering what we understand and forgetting what eludes us. Thus, the participants can share a common tendency toward selective inattention, unless listeners can discriminate wisely and know when something essential is missing. For example, some terminal patients are very reticent about disclosing how they feel and what they think about. No one disputes this observation. But if the reticence continues day after day with unwavering consistency, under every conceivable circumstance, then it is likely that something distinctive is being overlooked. Is the patient denying, or is he depressed, or too sick to care? What is he reticent about?

Selective inattention is a bias that omits evidence. So to counter its effect, we must devise ways of eliciting reasons for the omission and uniformity. First of all, we can ask patients almost anything: Why are you so reticent? What would you like to say to me? How can we help you more? We can get information from the family or staff nurses; we can find out about drug reactions that might stupefy a patient and make him more reticent than usual. Selective inattention will, of course, prevent the worker from asking just these questions, as if he already knows the answers.

Overgeneralization is easy to recognize: a patient is said always or never to do something; he is assumed to have unequivocal reasons for saying, feeling, or acting in an unambiguous manner. There are no problems in reaching a conclusion from the reporter's standpoint. "Mr. A. never complained. He was always cheerful, joked a lot, and we all liked him. I don't think he realized how sick he was, because he never asked, even at his worst, when he just waved us away." In other words, the patient was never morose or worried; if he didn't joke, he was silent. And no one seems to have inquired about his inner state (a statement which itself is a good example of overgeneralization). During the psychological autopsy, we suspect that a reporter generalizes immoderately if he seems to get too much mileage out of minimal information and tells us little about the words *behind* the patient's words.

Impressions vs. Analysis

What is retrospective reconstruction—that ringing phrase that recurs so often during this book? Reconstruction of what? What is the process of retrospecting and reconstructing?

The psychological autopsy has had at least as many critics as advocates, if it is known or practiced at all. Aside from suicidologists, however, few investigators have used the procedure often enough to be regarded as supporters or detractors. There can be little doubt but that the psychological autopsy has many problems pertaining to reliability and validity of constructs as well as data. Despite my own recognition of how easily information can be misconstrued and overlooked, leading to erroneous conclusions, these and other difficulties—reliance upon authority and consensus— are not insurmountable. The method itself has sufficient merit to encourage further trial, experimentation, introduction of other data-gathering techniques, better-trained personnel, in different clinical settings.

The gripping anecdote and glib report command attention. They may also inspire useless generalities. How shall we balance global impressions of total situations with systematic analysis of selected behavior?

Our major purpose, aside from retrospective reconstruction, is to develop uniform methods for assessing patients, which trained and compassionate observers can then apply with minimal distortion, and with evenhanded relevance, specificity, and generality. This noble-enough goal is almost certainly unreachable.

We must begin with the observer, and with his shortcomings. Anyone can make an observation, selecting and rejecting perceptions, uttering conclusions, mistaking prejudices for principles. There is no substitute for the confidence that admits ignorance; this is the prerequisite for observers who would recognize their own misconceptions and mistakes.

The geriatric version of the psychological autopsy showed that untrained but concerned participants can contribute substantially to the reconstruction of the terminal phase. Their impressions could stand by themselves, but at the same time, we needed the experience and structure that training provides. The key issue is the observer—but this is a problem found in education in general. Students bring their own interest, and can become even more interested when they accumulate information and develop skills of their own. Impressions are useful for their own sake, but also because they provide hypotheses for systematic evaluation. Patients may be too sick, sedated, defensive, or inarticulate to be clear about themselves. We cannot fault them for being inconsistent, taciturn, truculent, or tired. We can blame trained observers who do not consider these factors relevant for their judgments and reports.

The art of relevance is not easily taught. We like to find what we already know, and assume that what we know is relevant. Nevertheless, assuming this can lead to more detailed tests and investigation, and to melding intuitions and impressions with itemizations and analyses.

We distinguish between *primary observations* (what the observer actually sees, hears, smells, feels, does, and makes sense out of) and *secondary constructions* (what the observer does about his direct observations). This is not the customary, but academic, distinction between data and inferences. Psychosocial situations seldom lend themselves to nice numerical ordering and objective categorization of what are data and what are inferences.

Psychosocial events cannot be taken out of context, and examined in meticulous isolation. Statements of and about patients must be put into a perspective before being evaluated. Often the perspective is implicit in the reports, but it resists disclosure.

This unfamiliar distinction between primary observations and secondary constructions proves far more practical in effect than vainly dissecting masses of verbal and nonverbal information into data and inferences. The practicality of separating observations from constructions lies in the fact that we can more readily distinguish between our perceptions and interpretations of what is immediately given and the policies and procedures we follow as a result. What we do is an implementation of how we interpret and "average out" a variety of perceptions. Collectively, our actions, verbal and nonverbal, are a policy which reasonably alert observers can detect, and, if they choose, dissect and dispute.

What are called *reports* in the psychological autopsy are perceptions and interpretations, i.e., primary observations. The subsequent discussion which emerges largely reconstructs the implicit policies and strategies used by both patient and staff, i.e., secondary constructions. The pivotal problem, of course, is to find out what exactly the observer saw, when it occurred, and what sense was made out of it. These perceptions are, in fact, low-level interpretations, implying a perspective that the autopsy itself must clarify. Moreover, low-level interpretations are the building blocks for secondary and tertiary constructions, even for the wisdom we later promulgate as "principles."

Here is an example of how perceptions and policies are interwoven: A nurse reports that a patient on her service is *afraid* of death. When asked for her data, she concedes that the patient simply lies quietly, somewhat tense, uncomplaining, without asking for additional medication. He answers questions briefly, is not withdrawn, and has never mentioned death. Why does she then think he is afraid of death? This would imply that he both knows the prognosis and is apprehensive. Further discussion discloses that she believes that anyone who faces certain death must be afraid. Therefore, the less they say, the more accepting they seem, the more defended they must be. In short, she leaves no room for the patient who actually accepts the reality of dying without fear. She, too, fears death and cannot speak about it, so her report is not a perception but a statement of how she interprets whatever occurs. The secondary construction or policy is implicit: she is supportive, reassuring, helpful, and fortifies denial whenever it can be found. She divides serious illness into multiple treatable procedures, and in exchange, expects her patient to be uncomplaining and not to bring up unpleasant subjects.

The physician in charge recalls that shortly after arriving at a definitive diagnosis and treatment plan, he spoke with the patient. But he notes that the patient asked nothing about the prognosis, and since their early conversation, has sought and been given no further information, even during the recent period of decline. The patient goes on, day after day, mildly responsive, but generally apathetic and disinterested. He does not protest or challenge anything, whether the treatment or his persistent symptoms. The doctor assumes that somehow the patient is aware of the outlook, although he has not indicated as much. Nevertheless, because the patient seems so indifferent to whether he leaves the hospital or stays on indefinitely, and fails to show any sign of anxiety, the physician concludes that his patient is *depressed*.

The doctor's primary observations are clear: apathy, disinterest, inactivity, failure to complain, no overt dejection, weeping, or hopelessness. His policy, based upon secondary constructions, is to avoid open confrontation with patients because this might lead to further depression. This is obviously a circular argument, but it is not logic that concerns us here. The doctor's policy and implementation are based upon treatment of depression: careful attention to physical needs, unilateral and benevolent decisions, daily encouragement without pressuring the patient toward more activity, no talk about the future, scrutiny of the chart, conspicuous readjustment of equipment, hearty self-confidence.

The patient's wife does not agree that her husband is either anxious or depressed. In the first place, he has not spoken about dying. He wants to go home when he's ready, but prefers to leave this decision to the doctor, believing that when the time comes, he will be told. In fact, his main topic whenever she calls, which is almost daily, concerns the children. How are they? What are they doing about school? She tells him about people who call or telephone, and he brightens up a bit, rambles on about rehabilitation and ultimately return-ing to work. His wife knows, of course, that the future is bleak, that these are brave words spoken through the mist of illusion, but she cannot bring herself to say that he is not coming home and will never go back to work. She and the caseworker have discussed practical prob-lems for the future—a job, another place to live, what to say to the children. She has the belief that her husband actually is unaware of his plight, that he is therefore not afraid, and depressed only because he is unable to be at home, buoying her spirits and taking care of their family.

Assuming that the wife's report is correct, is the patient denying facts or implications about his fatal illness? Or does he recognize his condition rightly, but dissimulates because that is all he can offer to his distressed wife? The facts are not as crucial as our ability to distinguish between the wife's primary obser-vations, how she sees her husband and interprets his remarks and attitude, and her policy with respect to what goes on during daily visits. Her policy is geared to denial and mutual support—denial of the future, pre-tense that all will be well, distraction through detailed accounts of visitors and their get-well wishes.

The psychiatrist is puzzled. At first, he and the patient got along very well. But now the patient is becoming more and more remote and surly. He may turn away. Once he said, "What good does it do to talk about things that can't be changed?" If the psychiatrist persists, he is apt to be rewarded with curt, concrete, and monosyllabic answers. The patient seems either antagonistic or indifferent. Recently, the patient asked the psychiatrist not to come back, an act that both embarrassed and saddened the latter.

These are some of the psychiatrist's primary observations. His secondary construction or policy follows his awareness of becoming *persona non grata*. He concludes that the patient is feeling endangered by his illness or by the psychiatric inquiry. He finds no sign of anxiety, denial, or depression, but much evidence of hostility. The psychiatrist elaborates his constructions. Perhaps the patient's anger and endangerment stem from helplessness and incapacity, and not from being irked at the psychiatrist himself. If this hypothesis is true, the patient's anger is the primary observation. Hostility, a more general state, resulting from helplessness, futility, frustration, and incapacity, is the secondary construction. What does the psychiatrist do about it? This question, of course, is equally pertinent for anyone else involved in a patient's care. Policies and procedures may reflect not only personal attitudes toward a patient, but perceptions of the patient's impact.

During a psychological autopsy, we might inquire about the psychiatrist's personal feelings. Is he becoming more frustrated, helpless, and incapable of pursuing earlier plans? If so, perhaps he mirrors the patient's attitude. Maybe he is getting angry, but fails to mention his personal feelings in his report. How can one get angry at patients who are hopelessly ill? However, if this is not acknowledged, the hostility may show itself in other ways. ("How did I feel about the patient? Well, I expected him to be more appreciative. Did I do something wrong? I don't think so, although I might have done something different. Anyway, why don't I leave well enough alone . . . just peek in once in awhile. After all, I can't force him to talk.")

The policy is clear. Mutual hostility generates isolation and distance. Despair is hard to admit without also conveying blame, incapacity, anger. These sentiments interpret our psychiatrist's interpretations, and as such participate in the future policies we use to ameliorate what seems to be a standoff.

The psychologist who tested the patient finds that, despite physical deterioration, the patient is cooperative, articulate, and while not very productive, is certainly not confused. His score on the POMS shows high tension and vigor, low depression, confusion, and anger. While the POMS is a self-rating test, the psychologist found no clear evidence to contradict the patient. In fact, his findings dispute the conclusions drawn by the previous reporters. Major themes in the TAT concern desertion, reconciliation, intimacy, and disappointment. And as the psychological reports are being given, each participant in the autopsy scans the material for confirmation or contradiction. The psychologist discovered no further evidence of denial, anxiety, or depression, indicating either that his tests were not sensitive enough or the other observers misconstrued events. How to explain this discrepancy? The tests were done very early in the patient's hospital course. Aha! Depression, denial, anxiety developed later. But no—they were repeated one week ago, with the same results. Well, by that time, someone says, the patient was beyond caring, even beyond depression. What were the responses to the so-called "death" cards on the TAT? Not remarkable. Just the same as earlier.

Who is right and who is wrong? What is really going on? The psychological autopsy recognizes that there is no secret truth that underlies and measures every report, giving it a score. The very process of illness and sickness unto death suggests that every report has an intrinsic validity. But this does not mean that one report is as good as another, and therefore no documentation or analysis is necessary.

The time factor is critical, of course. *When* an observation is made is as important as the nature of the perception itself. If we think of a course of illness like an uncertain railroad timetable, then we cannot rely *entirely* upon what the clock says if we want to know where we are. Other evidence is needed, and if different passengers have conflicting perceptions, then there should be other ways to establish place and position. The difference between a retrospective reconstruction and a prospective railroad timetable is that passengers vary in how vividly and tendentiously they recall each intermediate town and village. The psychological autopsy, correctly applied, will find ways to check and correct inconsistencies. But we are also prepared for persistent and never-to-be-established certainty. Practitioners of the autopsy learn that we all stand within unspecified circumstances much of the time. We walk through a hall of mirrors, confronting and correcting ourselves, yet finding continuity enough from one image to the next to find our way.

Until we fully appreciate that the core of existence consists of ambiguity, anxiety, and ambivalence, we will search for some vain certainty or system that simply cannot be found. However, we deal with uncertainty by correcting mistakes and reinterpreting policies. Impressions and analyses are not different procedures, but different settings for our perceptions.

The extended example of how different professionals construe the behavior of one fatally ill patient demonstrates that (1) if we limited our observations to what the patient actually said and did, we would find he didn't say or do very much, (2) our confusion would be based upon inner expectations that whatever we perceived had an abiding reality, and (3) what we said or thought had an inner truth. We should also remember that (4) validity consists of what we believe as well as perceive, and (5) reliability is a product of psychosocial forces, lending meaning and motion to what we make sense out of and do about it.

Policies are difficult to recognize without careful construction of interpersonal events and trends. How people cope with problems never represents a uniform process. We cannot assume that our interpretation is either that of the patient or correct at all times. We seek an inner consistency, looking for a style or psychological setting. Perhaps the closest analogy is to compare the perceptions of a reporter who selects different phases of an event for his news story, with the interpretations of an editorial writer who uses various trends of different stories to arrive at a general interpretation and construction.

Coping and Vulnerability

Ironically, data which can be measured most easily and unequivocally are often least relevant. Furthermore, specific and isolated episodes may be most difficult to analyze without complete knowledge of overall circumstances. For example, we might count the visitors, measure how long they stayed, determine the relationship of each visitor to the patient. LeShan noticed how often dying patients rang for the floor nurse and how promptly she responded. But all that the actual number of visitors tell us is that a patient was not abandoned. The conversations are unrecorded, and the significance of each contact is undetermined.

How people actually cope with problems can either be overly specific, bordering on the idiosyncratic, or so general as to mean very little. There is no index of human behavior. Coping itself is a goal-directed process related to defined problems, and is intended to bring about relief, reward, quiescence, and equilibrium. In ordinary language, coping is simply regarded as a successful or unsuccessful resolution, without too much attention given to the strategies used. The slate of defense mechanisms usually promulgated is too general for practical application, especially when we consider how people cope with different problems, with varying effectiveness, over time. To be useful, general coping strategies should be formulated in terms of *intermediate generality*, neither too broad nor too narrow. Their significance emerges only when the predominant strategy can be correlated with a list of predominant concerns, with a corresponding appraisal of how successful resolution has been, and with the measure of difficult coping, which we term vulnerability. Table 4 gives a list of *General Coping Strategies*, under which more specific defensive and adaptive measures can be subsumed. The *Index of Vulnerability* is an effort to detect types of difficulty that patients encounter in the

Table 4.   General Coping Strategies

Problem:
1. What did you do (or are doing) about it?

_____ 1. Find out more before acting [Rational investigation]

_____ 2. Talk it over with someone to relieve distress [Share concern]

_____ 3. Laugh it off, see humor in the situation [Reversal of affect]

_____ 4. Try to forget, don't worry, wait and see [Suppression/isolation/detachment]

_____ 5. Put mind on other things, do something for distraction, carry on, business as usual [Displacement/diversion]

_____ 6. Carry out positive action based on present understanding [Confrontation/negotiation]

_____ 7. Rise above it, accept the situation, find something favorable or encouraging, make virtue out of necessity [redefinition/rationalization/reinterpretation]

_____ 8. Submit to the inevitable, stoic acceptance of the worst [Passivity/fatalism]

_____ 9. Do something, anything, however ambiguous, impractical, reckless, irrelevant, or magical [Acting out/impulsive acts/compulsive rituals]

_____10. Consider alternatives based on past situations [Rigid or uncorrected repetition]

_____11. Drain off or reduce tension with eating, smoking, drinking, drugs, etc. [Tension relief by physiological means]

_____12. Get away from it all, phantasy or pretend for purpose of relief [Social withdrawal/stimulus reduction/avoidance]

_____13. Blame someone or something, disown responsibility, get angry [Projection/externalization]

_____14. Comply, do what I'm told, yield to authority, seek direction [Adopt a role/obedience/compliance]

_____15. Blame self, atone, sacrifice [Masochistic sur-
render]
2. How did it work (or is working) out?
_____ 1. No resolution at all
_____ 2. Uncertain, indefinite, doubtful resolution
_____ 3. Qualified resolution
_____ 4. Conclusive, definite resolution
3. What do you think you should have done?
_____ 0. Just what I did
_____ 1. Something else, which would be ____ (No.)
4. What do you think others would have done, given the same
problem?
_____ 0. Just what I did
_____ 1. Something else, which would be ____ (No.)

* This scheme is based on an outline first suggested by Sidle et al (Arch. Gen.
Psychiatry, 20:2 (1969), 226-232)

process of coping. Semantics being what it is, vul-
nerabilities consist of thirteen polarities of mood, attitude, or behavior found to be most prevalent and
readily observable among terminal or suicidal patients.
Note that each item is matched with its opposite in
order to minimize ambiguity in understanding what
each means. There are six degrees of difference which
the observer-rater decides about, ranging from High,
High moderate, Low moderate, to Least, with other
choices between (Table 5).

The classification of *Predominant Concerns* is simply a convenient way to tabulate the major field of
action that a patient seeks to cope with and may be
especially vulnerable to. Health, work/finances, family,
friends, religion, self-appraisal, and existential concerns
are categories which can be replaced readily with
others, provided that they can be defined well enough to
be used by several observers.

Table 5. Index of Vulnerability

1. Hopeless							Hopeful
Pt believes that all is lost, futile, no chance for recovery	6	5	4	3	2	1	Pt believes in brighter, better future, confident about recovery
2. Turmoil/perturbation							Controlled/composed
Pt is tense, agitated, restless, visibly distressed	6	5	4	3	2	1	Pt is placid, calm, seems in charge of emotions
3. Frustration							Relieved
Pt is angry about incapacity to resolve problems, to bring about relief, to get satisfaction	6	5	4	3	2	1	Pt feels problems are being resolved, pleased with present outcome
4. Despondent/depressed							Responsive/encouraged
Pt is extremely dejected, weeps, withdrawn, retarded, and inaccessible to others	6	5	4	3	2	1	Pt accepts interaction with others, relative well-being, reaches out
5. Helpless/powerless							Resourceful/autonomous
Pt feels incapable of initiating action on his/her behalf; complains of	6	5	4	3	2	1	Pt initiates actions to obtain relief, feels able to bring about constructive change

Table 5. Index of Vulnerability (Continued)

	6	5	4	3	2	1	
being too weak or over-powered to struggle							*Secure/confident* Pt feels able to contend with risk, danger, or uncertainty
6. *Anxiety/fears* Pt feels panic or dread, senses impending calamity, with annihilation	6	5	4	3	2	1	*Zestful/energetic* Pt has high energy level, enthusiastic, vigorous
7. *Exhaustion/apathy* Pt feels depleted; wants to feel better but too worn out to care much	6	5	4	3	2	1	*Self-esteem/high personal value* Continues to have good self-image, consistent with reality
8. *Worthless/self-rebuke* Pt feels no good, blames self for misfortunes, deserving nothing	6	5	4	3	2	1	*Feels cared for/secure* Pt is certain that support and affiliations will continue, that needs are being met satisfactorily
9. *Painful isolation/abandoned* Pt feels lonely, ignored, alienated, deserted	6	5	4	3	2	1	

Table 5.   Index of Vulnerability (Continued)

	6	5	4	3	2	1	
10. *Denial/avoidance* Pt speaks or acts in ways showing unwillingness or inability to recognize threatening implications							*Awareness/good reality-testing* Pt correctly perceives problems relating to illness, immediate and implicit
11. *Truculence/resentment* Pt is embittered about treatment or neglect, feels victimized							*Acceptance/appreciation* Pt recognizes facts about illness and treatment, that whatever outcome, efforts have been sustaining
12. *Repudiation of SKO* Pt rejects or antagonizes help or support, usually family/friend							*Mutuality with SKO* Pt maintains, accepts, initiates give-and-take supportive relationships
13. *Closed-time perspective* Pt foresees no tomorrow, unable to visualize any future							*Open-time perspective* Pt expects unlimited future even with residues of illness

Perhaps the most effective way to find out about coping strategies and vulnerability is to ask patients (1) What they did or are doing about a particular problem (placed under one of the predominant concerns)? (2) How did it work out? (3) What would others have done, given similar problems? (4) What they themselves might do over again, if they had a chance? and (5) What kept them from doing things that way in the first place?

Efforts to classify how patients contend with their concerns may be and probably are rather awkward and artificial. But without these efforts, whatever they are, we would be even more restricted to the private revelations of individual reporters, who are subject to the distortions I noted in the previous section. Comparison of one person with another is a cumbersome business at best. Until better instruments are devised, however, we can find a little consolation by recalling that a building can be appreciated as a structure, without knowing how to design a similar building or to use the materials that went into its construction. Furthermore a degree of familiarity with draftsmanship, architecture, engineering, and structural materials will help to establish a bridge between general artistic and aesthetic appreciation and itemized analyses of the cost accounting and contracting problems.

Life-Threatening Behavior

Suicide, attempted or completed, is the paradigm of intentional death. Although suicide is a form of life-threatening behavior, not all forms of life-threatening behavior are suicidal. Shneidman and many others have shown how people participate in bringing about their own demise, without overt intention to die. Menninger's classic *Man Against Himself* (1938) cited numerous examples of the triad he calls the wish to kill, to be killed, or to die.

Some life-threatening activities pertain to illness and injury, not merely to intention, as a factor in death. Therefore, the psychological autopsy concerns itself with life-threatening behavior, especially as it applies to hospitalized patients. It is, of course, true that a dangerous way of life may also be an affirmation of one's competence and self-reliance; the brush with death is an exhilarating event at times. But these stimulating circumstances usually require a state of good health rarely found among subjects for the psychological autopsy. We do find patients who defy regulations, break rules and regimens, and directly endanger themselves by imprudent behavior, without being suicidal. In their prehospital experience, these patients may also have shown considerable disdain or vulnerability about matters of deep and predominant concern.

For the purposes of the psychological autopsy, the following classification of life-threatening behavior has proved to be useful in striking the necessary balance of generality and specificity. In each category, our defining characteristic is that the patient carries out an action or series of acts deleterious to physical safety.

1. *Self-injury/intoxication*
   These are self-initiated, more or less infrequent acts resulting in trauma, poisoning, or pronounced intoxication. The category includes hard-drug usage, nonsuicidal ingestions and injuries (sufficient to require medical attention,

even if none is sought), and occasional abuse of alcohol.

2. *Rash, regretted, incautious, or bizarre acts*
These acts are clearly associated with impulsive behavior, very poor judgment, or serious psychiatric disturbances. They include reckless, unskilled use of potentially dangerous tools, vehicles, and implements of many kinds. Speeding on slippery highways, walking alone at night in dangerous neighborhoods, or even more conspicuous acts of jeopardy. Not included, however, is behavior which is simply immoral, undesirable, or embarrassing, unless physical risk is involved.

3. *Significant omissions*
These are instances of overt self-neglect in a *clinical setting*, e.g., procrastination in the presence of serious signs of physical illness, refusal to follow important recommendations for treatment, failure to persevere with significant diagnostic measures, omitting insulin, digitalis, or other life-conserving medications.

4. *Significant excesses*
These refer to types of behavior in which the frequency, intensity, or tenacity obviously endangers health and physical well-being, even though in milder forms such behavior might be quite harmless. Common examples are chronic alcoholism, gross gluttony, starvation diets, certain fads, excess tobacco, and mild psychedelic drug abuse.

5. *Countertherapeutic behavior*
These forms are exclusively found in hospitals,

where patients who are expected to conform to certain rules and roles compromise treatment and health by defying and undermining their own best interests. Regardless of provocation and justification, patients who are led to sign out against medical advice, refuse mandatory surgery, or terminate treatment as an act of rebellion may place themselves in a dangerous impasse.

Detailed analysis of life-threatening behavior is beyond the scope of this discussion of the psychological autopsy. This is fortunate for the author because it is often exceedingly difficult to decide whether a patient's unusual, aberrant, or assertive behavior and conduct threatens his physical health, or merely infringes our personal standards of how patients ought to comport themselves.

We cannot doubt, however, that certain types of behavior are life-threatening, and are more than an idiosyncratic example of a deviant life-style. In short, they are signs of endangerment anxiety, a common precursor of self-contributory death. Patients who exhibit such behavior are apt to be vulnerable in many ways. Although life-threatening behavior is not to be confused with so-called suicide equivalents in every instance, defective coping strategies may be found commonly among people who tend to be unusually brittle, sensitive, vindictive, or impulsive. The price of their nonconformity is prohibitively extravagant. In any event, whether a patient is suicidal or preterminal, a history of life-threatening behavior, as an isolated episode or a pattern of conduct, may be very revealing in retrospect. It offers a glimpse into the personality and psychosocial field of a patient who lived and died therein.

Presuicidal Period

Assessment of the presuicidal patient is one of the most elusive problems in clinical practice. It seems tautological to say that presuicidal thinking reflects high vulnerability. Lethality, the disposition to kill oneself, may be strong, even if the person fails to attempt suicide. Shneidman's outline for the psychological autopsy (Table 1) shows what to look for in reviewing the recent events in the life of a suicidal victim. Table 6 is an indication of relevant kinds of presuicidal information which helps to circumscribe the scope and severity of lethality. While many psychological tests and inventories have been proposed to detect the potential suicide, none has gained general acceptance. The reader is advised that presuicidal information may constitute important *clues* to a subsequent attempt, but it should not be considered *reasons* for the attempt, which usually escapes even our most intensive inquiries. Table 7, the Risk-Rescue Rating, outlines operational information related to an actual attempt.

Empathy and Explanation

The task of understanding the *realization of death* is the central focus of this book. It finds a paradigm in the psychological autopsy, but it may be found in almost

Table 6. Presuicidal Period

1. Duration of ideation

____0. None
____1. Less than 48 hrs.
____2. Less than 1 wk.
____3. Less than 1 mo.
____4. Less than 6 mos.
____5. Less than 1 yr.
____6. More than 1 yr.

2. Persistence of ideation

____1. No suicidal thoughts
____2. Occasional
____3. Frequent
____4. Near-constant

3. Specificity

____0. None or denied
____1. Vague/ambiguous
____2. Definite method in
       mind/arrangements

4. Advance planning

____0. None or denied
____1. Uncertain plans
____2. Elaborate plans

5. Plan to thwart rescue

____0. None
____1. Explicit

6. Hallucinations or delusions
   at or near focal attempt

____0. No
____1. Yes
       Specify _____
       _____

7. Degree of dissociation at
   or near focal attempt

____0. None
____1. Vague confusion
____2. Disorientation
____3. Psychotic

8. Overt suicidal threats

____0. None
____1. Implication only
____2. Specific

9. Ability to communicate
   distress

____0. None communicated
____1. Nonverbal only
____2. Direct and explicit

10. Significant other's response

____0. Ignored or denied problem
____1. Reassured
____2. Attempt to help and understand

11. Suicide note

____0. None
____1. Yes, to be found after death
____2. Yes, to be found before death

12. Contact with professionals
    during past month

____0. None
____1. Yes
       Specify_____

13. Terminal illness

____0. None
____1. Thought he/she had
____2. Yes
       Specify_____

14. Destructive ideation in past 1 mo.

____0. None
____1. Yes
       Toward?_____

15. Recent use of drugs/alcohol

____0. No
____1. Yes
       Specify_____

Table 7. Risk-Rescue Rating

Risk Score_____

Rescue Score_____

Risk-Rescue Rating_____ _____

atient _____ Age_____ Sex_____ Previous Attempts_____

ircumstances _____

_____

_____

_____

RISK FACTORS	RESCUE FACTORS

RISK FACTORS

1. Agent used:

___1 Ingestion, cutting, stabbing
___2 Drowning, asphyxiation,
       strangulation
___3 Jumping, shooting

2. Impaired consciousness:

___1 None in evidence
___2 Confusion, semicoma
___3 Coma, deep coma

3. Lesions/Toxicity:

___1 Mild
___2 Moderate
___3 Severe

4. Reversibility:

___1 Good, complete recovery
       expected
___2 Fair, recovery expected with
       time
___3 Poor, residuals expected,
       if recovery

5. Treatment required:

___1 First aid, E.W. care
___2 House admission, routine
       treatment
___3 Intensive care, special
       treatment

otal Risk Points_____

RISK SCORE

. High risk   (13-15 risk points)
. High moderate   (11-12 risk points)
. Moderate   (9-10 risk points)
. Low moderate   (7-8 risk points)
. Low risk   (5-6 risk points)

RESCUE FACTORS

1. Location:

___3 Familiar
___2 Non-familiar, non-remote
___1 Remote

2. Person initiating rescue:*

___3 Key person
___2 Professional
___1 Passerby

3. Probability of discovery by
    any rescuer:

___3 High, almost certain
___2 Uncertain discovery
___1 Accidental discovery

4. Accessibility to rescue:

___3 Asks for help
___2 Drops clues
___1 Does not ask for help

5. Delay until discovery:

___3 Immediate 1 hour
___2 Less than 4 hours
___1 Greater than 4 hours

Total Risk Points_____

RESCUE SCORE†

1. Least rescuable   (5-7 rescue points)
2. Low moderate   (8-9 rescue points)
3. Moderate   (10-11 rescue points)
4. High moderate   (12-13 rescue points)
5. Most rescuable   (14-15 rescue points)

* Self-rescue automatically yields a Rescue Score of 5.
† If there is undue delay in obtaining treatment after
   discovery, reduce the final Rescue Score by one point.

any other form of creative, investigative, or constructive endeavor. Novels, plays, poetry, philosophical essays, religious tracts, and strictly physiological determinations can all reveal something about how dying and death are made real and realizable to mankind.

In an earlier section, *"Impressions vs. Analysis,"* I discussed the theoretical foundation for the psychological autopsy method, if it is to be used as a feasible instrument. I stressed the awareness, alertness, and acumen of the observer-reporter, who perceives and implements policies, often implicitly, and then, with the assistance of other participants, measures various items, examines coping strategies, and decides about a patient's vulnerability.

Impressions and analysis are necessary for the method. The investigator needs a balance of enlightened empathy and intelligible explanation. We can explain without understanding, and understand without being able to explain. We can glibly intellectualize about motivated behavior, and impose cavalier reasons that make sense to us, but without really sensing why people act and feel as they do.

Explanations use theories and hypotheses. Understanding depends upon a sense of reality and of relevance. Together, they establish coherence and common denominators between lived-in experience and events which at first seem dissimilar. For example, we can understand someone's thirst, because we have been thirsty. We know that a drink of water relieves thirst, even though we may not be thirsty at the moment. However, it is more difficult to explain thirst, unless we already know about mucous membranes, fluid bal-

ance, water and sodium depletion, and the hypo-
thalamus.

The psychological autopsy uses understanding of
behavior, explanations of certain events, empathy with
the patient, and theories which help to explain further.
In short, the exercise combines the personal and the
professional in every participant. Each person is called
upon to listen and to use his or her knowledge. But in
addition participants share sentiments, memories, reflections, and appreciation of the existential episode
itself.

The personal and professional elements fuse, because we talk of our meetings *with* the patient and *about*
the patient. The personal phase is the *encounter*. One
person meets another at a moment of high vulnerability. It is an interface between them, and most often
takes place on a kind of "precipice," beyond the scope of
treatment and beyond the factual knowledge of the
professional. The concomitant professional phase is the
evaluation. The observer organizes his information according to methods and operations used in order to
reach a measure of explanation—what can be made
real, what can be done about it?

It is usually beyond the skill of clinicians to convey
fully the depth of anguish, or the scope of a patient's
courage. Some human feelings, if not all, are so private
that we cannot adequately evaluate them without being
overly subjective or crassly intellectual. Nevertheless,
the professional who has realized the encounter as a
living fact will also find that empathy broadens understanding, and in doing so, advances toward a unified
explanation.

Despite appearances, the combined use of the existential and the operational is not a fuzzy notion. It is a common event. Say we want to decide whether someone we know is an honest man. On one hand, we can simply declare our feeling that he is a good person, straightforward in his dealings, frank, compassionate, and perceptive. With these virtues, we guess that he is not likely to be deceptive or to take undue advantage of another person. Our empathy taps into his existence, which we judge to be authentic enough to call him an honest man.

On the other hand, we can look for operational criteria for honesty, so that we can evaluate this man's honesty as empirically as we measure his height, weight, or social position. According to these standards, an honest man does not steal, cheat, lie, or deprive other people of their property. He does not do illicit things.

Existentially, this man is deemed honest because he reflects standards which have a directive, not just a prohibitive, significance. Our interface is so direct and generates so much trust that honesty is self-evident. We might be wrong. But our explanation of his honesty is consistent with everything else we know and feel about him. Operationally, this man would be considered honest in that he has not advocated or practiced illegal acts as his general policy.

This example is relevant because we look for *typifying instances* which convey both an impression and a theory about a person's life-style and death-style. We use both empathy and explanation, because our job is to understand how a patient perceives his world, and to infer the policies he uses in his key relationships. Extreme or unusual events are not, as a rule, typifying instances. Our judgments, therefore, depend upon a kind of averaging over time, just as an honest man can be expected to have moments when he might be devious or deceptive, without destroying our overall confidence in him.

Social Judgments About Death

Ultimately, realization of how someone approaches death brings everyone to think about the human predicament itself, the common denominator of dying or intending to die. Our understanding of psychosocial forces depends to a large extent upon social judgment, the beliefs and standards we hold. These are our personal guidelines for whatever makes life desirable, absurd, tragic, significant, or deplorable. If living and dying are but two phases of the same process, then the death or near-death of a patient will evoke a realization that we share part of the focal event.

I wondered earlier how a deceased person might regard himself, were he to appear at an autopsy. Could we ask him if he died a "good" death? How might he have coped more effectively with his predominant concerns? In what way was he vulnerable? The final question is what have we learned from him and through him? Could we have made his death more acceptable and appropriate?

The psychological autopsy always has this invisible witness. His presence can even be used as a psychodramatic device by asking him questions and role-playing his responses. Apart from this, however, the witness is there when we turn to the *retrospective questions*, examples of which are given on pages 33-34.

Social judgments about death are evaluations of the quality or desirability of death, or of the situation that led to a suicide attempt. The evaluation also is a judgment as to our interventions, actual or imagined, in the past or in the future. We try not to be too idealistic or visionary. The accomplishments of psychosocial intervention can easily be overestimated. However, just as a regular autopsy can reveal something that will help solve problems in other cases, so, too, with the aims of the psychological autopsy. Here are some feasible objectives:

1. Adequate medical care, alleviation of pain and suffering, full use of technical resources, prolongation of life, but not prolongation of dying when recovery is wholly out of the question.
2. Informed consent, or, even better, informed collaboration between doctor and patient.
3. Encouragement of conscious, competent control, helping the patient to use available, practical, and appropriate coping strategies.
4. Maintenance of behavior on as high a level as seems consistent with physical and psychological limitations.
5. Preservation and, if necessary, enhancement of self-esteem, which is an essential ingredient of a dignified death.
6. Support of the significant key others, a gesture which helps them to help the patient.
7. Gradual relinquishment of control to those who

have shown themselves to be trustworthy and acceptance of counter-control.
8. Safe conduct in sustaining life until it ceases.
9. Honest communication, designed to support acceptance, reduce bitterness, and replace denial with courage to confront what cannot be changed.

Promises and Potential

The problems facing the psychological autopsy are not insoluble. We need to acquire the experience and intelligence to balance discipline and flexibility, using such information as we have to formulate answerable questions. Once again, however, behind tangible data, explicit methodology, standards of validity, and careful objectivity, is the observer-participant-reporter-policy maker. Both promises and potential are products of people.

The promises are that we can understand more about thanatology, the study of death-related situations and life-threatening behavior. Death is both a fact of nature, and an outcome of social forces. Societies, large and small, can be formulated as a phase of illness. When the illness is fatal or near-fatal, we may need an autopsy, namely, a systematic overview of ourselves, of which a patient represents a concrete example.

I have described but one form of this overview, called the psychological autopsy. It is not to be followed rigidly, but to be used as a guide. Consequently, it will evolve, along with more information and enlightened realization of how death and dying interdigitate with life and living. The terminal phase of life is but a confluence of forces set in motion long before.

Thanatology can be encouraged by the example of geriatric studies. Not too long ago, growing older was thought to be almost equivalent to becoming senile. All we knew was the pathology of old age. Nowadays, gerontology is a distinct discipline, and we scarcely need to remind anyone that growing older is part of being alive in the first place. We should not need to demonstrate that people confronted with death from any cause deserve to be heard and heeded. Serious illness, like some suicide attempts, is not always taken seriously enough. If cure is impossible, then care and safe conduct ensure a dignified exitus. It is our mutual obligation.

Realization of the common denominators of death requires acceptance of our own mortality. The psychological autopsy is but a protoscientific instrument for focusing on this basic fact.

The potential for the psychological autopsy is given by the amazing insistence on the part of the clergy, nursing profession, social work, and hospital administrators that more and more information and practical guidance be provided. Courses, seminars, and conferences are only a few indications of this trend. With few exceptions, physicians have not yet heard the message. Younger physicians and medical students, as well as older, especially the retired physicians, do realize that thanatology has been a conspicuous omission.

More recent graduates become aware with their earliest clinical experience that they cannot be exempted from considerations of death, dying, and self-destruction. Their generation knows the potential for annihilation and alienation in society, and in response, recognizes that those who are healthy need to protect the rights of others. Older doctors also recognize that freedom to live requires freedom to die with dignity. It is a basic right, which years of experience, coupled with their own aging, show to be one of the dimensions of being alive.

Who will perform psychological autopsies in the future? Psychiatrists should realize that preoccupation with mortality is not necessarily morbid or pathological. Thoughts about death and even about suicide as a solution are feasible methods of coping with problems. They are perhaps not very effective strategies, but not everything in psychiatry makes sense, anyway. I single out psychiatry as a logical candidate for leading the psychological autopsy because this discipline comes flush against the drive to survive, the intractibility of some human sufferings, the futility of living at all, and the inevitability of death. However, it is the rare psychiatrist who engages in this work, largely, I assume, because his sights are on a remote horizon, chasing rainbows in some respects. He fails to see that the darker side of human nature, like night itself, has its own secrets to explore, and that we can also see the stars, as well.

Psychologists, as a rule, are far better equipped than psychiatrists to discover better methods of studying death. Unfortunately, the social structure of medicine allows clinical psychologists only limited access to critically ill patients. In contrast, nurses and social workers have almost limitless contact. If they choose, they can be with patients and families around the clock. However, their training and tradition emphasize service, not research. This situation will certainly change, too.

Nurses are now recruited and trained for highly complex, intensive-care work. By the very nature of the patients they care for, skill in thanatology is also necessary. It is therefore reasonable for nurses to demand and receive instruction in psychosocial care. Problems connected with the dying and of the bereaved usually fall upon them, anyway. The advent of the nurse-clinician or the nurse who specializes in patient information is an optimistic omen.

Social workers have long since changed from their earlier status of ancillary professionals to that of cotherapists in psychiatry. The next step will be to use social service for further psychosocial investigations, since social workers already have interviewing skills beyond most physicians, and need only more theoretical training to become practical sociologists in hospitals.

What about physicians themselves? The enthusiasm with which some hospitals have embraced the Problem-Oriented Record may spread to psychosocial problems, too. Nevertheless, research into the actual mechanisms of dying is sketchy, and there are still many physicians of experience and goodwill who believe that they can contend with death-related situations without special interest or investigation. Recent emphasis and discussion about human studies, while currently concentrating on informed consent, may encourage medical scientists to find out more about why people die when they do. When this happens, they may also find out that kindness, support, and compassion are qualities not easily achieved, nor are they enough for improving the quality of death.

The potential for the psychological autopsy method is great. Good intentions, however, and homiletics about dignified death and safe conduct are not a substitute for clinical experience. But we also know that experience is sometimes the excuse we give for our mistakes and omissions. The anatomical autopsy implicitly holds doctors responsible for their perceptions, policies, and practice. The psychological autopsy might aspire to the same influence. First we need to translate clinical anecdotes into general principles. Psychosocial information is there, waiting to have relevant questions asked of it.

Other methods of realizing death are also feasible. The major purposes of the psychological autopsy, regardless of who participates, is to demystify death and dying, to explore death-related situations, without installing yet another mystique or mythology. A final word of guidance and caution: the search for human factors and forces in death and dying is like an ancient Chinese box puzzle. Each box has a secret spring that opens the cover to reveal another box. This box, too, holds a smaller box, which also has another box inside. Then there is another and another, until the last box is found. When this is opened, there is a tightly folded note, reading (in very small print, of course), "To whom it may concern: this puzzle cannot be solved."

REFERENCES

Chapter 1. Introduction

Brim, O., H. Freeman, S. Levine and N. Scotch (eds.). *The Dying Patient*. New York: Russell Sage Foundation, 1970.

Choron, J. *Modern Man and Mortality*. New York: The Macmillan Company, 1964.

Feifel, H. (ed.). *The Meaning of Death*. New York: McGraw-Hill Book Company, 1959.

Fulton, Robert (ed.). *Death and Identity*. New York: John Wiley & Sons, Inc., 1965.

Kastenbaum, Robert, and R. B. Aisenberg. *The Psychology of Death*. New York: Springer Publishing Company, 1972.

Parkes, C. Murray. *Bereavement: Studies of Grief in Adult Life*. New York: International Universities Press, Inc., 1972.

Shneidman, Edwin S. *Deaths of Man*. New York: Quadrangle/New York Times Book Company, 1973.

Vernick, Joel. *Selected Bibliography on Death and Dying*. Washington, D.C.: Information Office, National Institute of Child Health and Human Development, U.S. Department of Health, Education and Welfare, 1971.

Weber, F. *Aspects of Death and Correlated Aspects of Life in Art, Epigram, and Poetry: Contributions Towards an Anthology and an Iconography*. 4th ed. London: H. K. Lewis & Company, Ltd., 1922.

Weisman, Avery D. *On Dying and Denying: A Psychiatric Study of Terminality.* New York: Behavioral Publications, 1972.

Chapter 2. Principles

Ackerknecht, Erwin H. "Death in the History of Medicine," *Bulletin of the History of Medicine,* **42** (Jan.-Feb., 1968), 19–23.

Akiskal, Hagop S., and William T. McKinney, Jr. "Depressive Disorders: Toward a Unified Hypothesis," *Science,* **182** (1973), 20–29.

Allen, Nancy. *Suicide in California, 1960–1970.* State of California, Department of Public Health, 1973.

Bjorn, John C., and Harold D. Cross. *The Problem-Oriented Private Practice of Medicine: A System for Comprehensive Health Care.* Chicago: Modern Hospital Press, McGraw-Hill Publications Company, 1970.

Duff, R., and A. Hollingshead. *Sickness and Society.* New York, Ebbingsdon; and London: Harper & Row, 1968.

Farberow, Norman L., and E. S. Shneidman. *The Cry for Help.* New York: McGraw-Hill Book Company, 1961.

Feinstein, Alvan R. *Clinical Judgment.* Baltimore: Williams & Wilkins Company, 1967.

———. "A New Staging System for Cancer and Reappraisal of 'Early' Treatment and 'Cure' by Radical Surgery," *New England Journal of Medicine,* **249** (Oct. 3, 1968), 747–753.

Goldfinger, Stephen. "Case Records of the Massachusetts General Hospital (Case 27-1971)," *New England Journal of Medicine,* **285** (1971), 103–113.

Hackett, Thomas, and Avery D. Weisman. "Psychiatric Management of Operative Syndromes: I. The Therapeutic Consultation and the Effect of Noninterpretive Intervention," *Psychosomatic Medicine,* **22** (July-Aug., 1960), 267–282.

Krumbhaar, E. B. "History of the Autopsy and Its Relation to the Development of Modern Medicine," *Hospitals,* **12**:4 (1938), 68–74.

Osler, William. *Science and Immortality. The Ingersoll Lecture,*

1904. Cambridge: Houghton Mifflin Company, Riverside Press, 1904.

Park, Roswell. "Thanatology. A Questionnaire and a Plea for a Neglected Study," *Journal of the American Medical Association*, **63**:17 (April 27, 1912), 1243–1246.

Shneidman, Edwin S. "Suicide, Lethality, and the Psychological Autopsy," in *Aspects of Depression*, E. Shneidman and M. Ortega (eds.). International Psychiatry Clinics, Vol. 6, No. 2, pp. 225–250. Boston: Little, Brown & Company, 1969.

———— (ed.). *Essays in Self Destruction*. New York: Jason Aronson, Inc., 1967.

Sudnow, David. *Passing On: The Social Organization of Dying*. Englewood Cliffs, N.J.: Prentice Hall, Inc., 1967.

Weed, Lawrence L. *Medical Records, Medical Education, and Patient Care: The Problem-Oriented Record as a Basic Tool*. Cleveland: The Press of Case Western Reserve University, 1970 [Distributed by Year Book Medical Publishers, 35 East Wacker Drive, Chicago, Ill.].

————. "CPC's as Educational Instruments." *New England Journal of Medicine*, **285**:2 (1971), 115–118.

Weisman, Avery D. "Thanatology," in *Comprehensive Textbook of Psychiatry*, A. Freedman, H. Kaplan, and B. Sadock (eds.). 2d ed. Baltimore: Williams & Wilkins Company, 1974, Chap. 28.2.

————. "The Psychological Autopsy and the Potential Suicide: A Method of Pre-Mortem Diagnosis," *Bulletin of Suicidology* (Dec., 1967), 15–24.

————, and Robert Kastenbaum. *The Psychological Autopsy: A Study of the Terminal Phase of Life*. Community Mental Health Monographs, No. 4. New York: Behavioral Publications, 1968.

Chapter 3. Procedures

Adler, G., and P. Myerson (eds.). *Confrontation in Psychotherapy*. New York: Jason Aronson, Inc., 1973.

Bermosk, L., and R. Corsini (eds.). *Critical Incidents in Nurs-*

ing. Philadelphia, London, & Toronto: W. B. Saunders Company, 1973.

Glaser, Barney G., and A. L. Strauss. *Awareness of Dying.* Chicago: Aldine Publishing Company, 1965.

————. *Time for Dying.* Chicago: Aldine Publishing Company, 1968.

Hamburg, David A., and John E. Adams. "A Perspective on Coping Behavior: Seeking and Utilizing Information in Major Transitions," *Archives of General Psychiatry,* **17** (Sept., 1967), 277–284.

Hinkle, Lawrence E., Jr., and Harold G. Wolff. "The Nature of Man's Adaptation to His Total Environment and the Relation of This to Illness," *Archives of Internal Medicine,* **99** (1957), 442–460.

Holland, Jimmie. "Psychologic Aspects of Cancer," in *Cancer Medicine,* J. Holland and E. Frei (eds.). Philadelphia: Lea & Febiger, 1973. Chap. 16-2, pp. 991–1021.

Janis, Irving L. *Psychological Stress.* New York: John Wiley & Sons, Inc., 1958.

Kroeber, Theodore C. "The Coping Functions of the Ego Mechanisms," in *The Study of Lives,* Robert White (ed.). New York: Atherton Press, 1963, pp. 178–198.

Verwoerdt, Adriaan, and James L. Elmore. "Psychological Reactions in Fatal Illness. I. The Prospect of Impending Death," *Journal of the American Geriatric Society,* **15**:1 (1967), 9–19.

Weisman, Avery D. "Psychosocial Considerations in Terminal Care," in *Psychosocial Aspects of Terminal Care,* B. Schoenberg, A. Carr, D. Peretz, and A. Kutscher (eds.). New York & London: Columbia University Press, 1972, pp. 162–172.

————, and T. P. Hackett. "Predilection to Death," *Psychosomatic Medicine,* **23** (1961), 232–255.

Chapter 4. Case Illustrations

Abram, Harry. "The Psychiatrist, the Treatment of Chronic Renal Failure, and the Prolongation of Life: III," *American Journal of Psychiatry,* **128** (1972), 1534–1539.

Beard, B. H. "The Quality of Life before and after Renal Transplantation," *Disorders of the Nervous System,* **32** (1971), 24–31.

Breed, Warren. "Five Components of a Basic Suicide Syndrome," *Life-Threatening Behavior,* **2**:1 (Spring, 1972), 3–18.

Engel, George L. "A Life Setting Conducive to Illness. The Giving-Up–Given-Up Complex," *Annals of Internal Medicine,* **69** (1968), 293–300.

Farberow, N. L., E. S. Shneidman, and C. V. Leonard. "Suicide among General Medical and Surgical Hospital Patients with Malignant Neoplasms," *New Physician,* **13** (1964), 6–12.

Farberow, N. L., S. Ganzler, F. Cutter, and D. Reynolds. "An Eight-Year Survey of Hospital Suicides," *Life-Threatening Behavior,* **1**:3 (Fall, 1971), 184–202.

Fawcett, Jan, Melitta Leff, and William E. Bunney, Jr. "Suicide. Clues from Interpersonal Communication," *Archives of General Psychiatry,* **21** (Aug., 1969), 129–137.

Feifel, Herman, Jeffrey Freilich, and Lawrence J. Hermann. "Death Fear in Dying Heart and Cancer Patients," *Journal of Psychosomatic Research,* **17** (1973), 161–166.

Godin, A. (ed.). *Death and Presence: The Psychology of Death and the Afterlife.* Brussels: Lumen Vitae Press, 1972.

Gordon, David. *Overcoming the Fear of Death.* Baltimore: Pelican Books, Inc., 1972.

Hinton, John. *Dying.* Baltimore: Penguin Books, Inc., 1967.

Kubler-Ross, Elisabeth. *On Death and Dying.* New York: The Macmillan Company, 1969.

Lipowski, Z. J. "Physical Illness, the Individual and the Coping Process," *Psychiatry in Medicine,* **1**:2 (1970), 91–102.

——— (ed.). *Advances in Psychosomatic Medicine: Psychosocial Aspects of Physical Illness, Vol. 8.* London & New York: S. Karger, 1972.

Saunders, Cicely. "The Management of Patients in the Terminal Stage," in *Cancer,* Ronald W. Raven (ed.), Vol. 6, Chap. 18, pp. 403–417. London: Butterworth & Company, Ltd., 1959.

Schmidt, C., S. Perlin, W. Townes, R. Fisher, and J. Shaffer. "Characteristics of Drivers Involved in Single-Car Accidents," *Archives of General Psychiatry*, **27** (1972), 800–803.

Shneidman, E. S. "Perturbation and Lethality as Precursors of Suicide," *Life-Threatening Behavior*, **1**:1 (Spring, 1971), 23–45.

Weisman, Avery D. "The Value of Denying Death," *Journal of Pastoral Psychology*, **23** (1972), 24–32.

———. "Is Suicide a Disease?" *Life-Threatening Behavior*, **1**:4 (Winter, 1971), 219–231.

———. "Misgivings and Misconceptions in the Psychiatric Care of Terminal Patients," *Psychiatry*, **33**:1 (Feb., 1970), 67–81.

———. "The Patient with a Fatal Illness—To Tell or Not to Tell," *Journal of the American Medical Association*, **201** (1967), 646–648.

———, and T. Hackett. "Denial as a Social Act," in *Psychodynamic Studies on Aging: Creativity, Reminiscing, and Dying.* New York: International Universities Press, Inc., 1967.

———, and J. W. Worden. "Risk-Rescue Rating in Suicide Assessment," *Archives of General Psychiatry*, **26** (1972), 553–560.

Worden, J. W., and R. Sterling-Smith. "Lethality Patterns in Multiple Suicide Attempts," *Life-Threatening Behavior*, **3**:2 (1973), 95–104.

Twenty-Four Hours a Day. Alcoholics Anonymous, Daytona Beach, Fla., Hazelden, Center City, Minn., Undated.

Chapter 5. Common Denominators of Death

Kastenbaum, R., and A. Weisman. "The Psychological Autopsy as a Research Procedure in Gerontology," in *Research Planning and Action for the Elderly*, D. Kent, R. Kastenbaum, and S. Sherwood (eds.), Chap. 14, pp. 210–217. New York: Behavioral Publications, 1972.

Lazarus, Richard S. *Psychological Stress and the Coping Process.* New York: McGraw-Hill Book Company, Inc., 1966.

Lettieri, Dan. "Suicide in the Aging: Empirical Prediction of Suicidal Risk among the Aging," *Journal of Geriatric Psychiatry,* **6**:1 (1973), 7–42.

Mechanic, David. "Response Factors in Illness: The Study of Illness Behavior," *Social Psychiatry,* **1**:1 (1966), 11–20.

Menninger, K. *Man Against Himself.* New York: Harcourt Brace Jovanovich, 1938.

Montgomery, D. Wayne (ed.). *Healing and Wholeness.* Richmond, Va.: John Knox Press, 1971.

Selye, H. *The Stress of Life.* New York: McGraw-Hill Book Company, Inc., 1956.

Shaffer, J., S. Perlin, C. Schmidt, and M. Himelfarb. "Assessment in Absentia. New Directions in the Psychological Autopsy," *Johns Hopkins Medical Journal,* **130** (1972), 308–316.

Sidle, A., R. Moos, J. Adams, and P. Cady. "Development of a Coping Scale," *Archives of General Psychiatry,* **20**:2 (1969), 226–232.

Weisman, Avery D. "Reality Sense and Reality Testing," *Behavioral Science,* **3** (1958), 228–261.

———. "Suicide, Death, and Life-Threatening Behavior," in *Suicide Prevention in the Seventies,* H. Resnik and B. Hathorne (eds.). Rockville, Md.: National Institute of Mental Health, DHEW Publ. No. (HSM) 72-9054, 1973, Chap. III ("Death and Self-Destructive Behaviors"), pp. 13–22.

———. "The Psychotherapeutic 'Encounter' and Clinical Research," in *Proceedings, Third World Congress of Psychiatry.* Montreal: McGill University Press, 1961.

———. *The Existential Core of Psychoanalysis: Reality Sense and Responsibility.* Boston: Little, Brown & Company, 1965.

INDEX